FINANCIAL STATEMEN

Summary Financial Statements
A Guide to Best Practice

FINANCIAL STATEMENTS SERIES

Summary Financial Statements
A Guide to Best Practice

Katharine Bagshaw

Accountancy Books
40 Bernard Street
London
WC1N 1LD
Tel: +44 (0)20 7920 8991
Fax: +44 (0)20 7920 8992
E-mail: info@accountancybooks.co.uk
Website: www.accountancybooks.co.uk

ISBN 1 84140 014 9

British Library Cataloguing-in-Publication Data
A catalogue record for this book is available from the British Library.

Typeset by RefineCatch Limited, Bungay, Suffolk
Printed in Great Britain by Livesey Limited, Shrewsbury, Shropshire

Contents

Acknowledgements

The author is grateful for the co-operation of the Company Secretaries and the Staff of the Rank Group plc, Unilever plc, Orange plc and National Power plc in the writing of Chapter 6 of this book.

Foreword

Summary financial statements are sent to many thousands of private shareholders every year. Private shareholders represent well over 90 per cent of the shareholders of many FTSE 100 companies and the production of summary financial statements is no longer restricted to the privatised utilities and banks. Summary financial statements are the principal and most effective means of communication between many companies and their private shareholders and companies go to considerable lengths to ensure that the right corporate messages are delivered. Increasingly, companies with a relatively small number of shareholders produce a summary financial statement, not as a cost-cutting exercise, but because they know that their shareholders are turned off by heavyweight annual reports. All the evidence shows that a short summary financial statement is far more likely to be opened and read than the average annual report.

In this book, the second in the *Financial Statements Series*, Katharine Bagshaw looks at the presentation of the summary financial statements of 20 FTSE 100 companies, she looks in detail at the summary financial statements of seven of those companies and she talks to four of them. She has set out the regulatory background in detail and has performed a detailed analysis of reporting trends. I therefore recommend this book to you as the only comprehensive guide to best practice in this increasingly important area.

J D Coombe
Finance Director – Glaxo Wellcome plc
October 1999

CHAPTER 1

Introduction

1.1 Wider share ownership

Many FTSE 100 companies voluntarily produce a separate summary financial statement designed to meet the particular needs of private shareholders despite the fact that private shareholders own less than five per cent of the capital of many such companies. One reason for this is the sheer number of private shareholders: private individuals with small shareholdings account for over 80 per cent of the shareholders of many large companies and their profile makes them an active and influential group. Those who attend annual general meetings are often retired, hold shares in several different companies and a significant number work or have worked in professional and managerial positions. They have their own pressure groups and sometimes have a higher public profile than the institutional investors. This body of shareholders exists partly as a result of the actions taken by the Government in the 1980s to encourage wider share ownership.

1.1.1 The need for summary financial statements

The history of the summary financial statement produced by listed companies is fairly short. The mass privatisations of the 1980s and the consequential increase in share ownership in sections of the population that had not previously owned shares meant that the annual report was being received and read by a much wider audience than had previously been the case. The existing regulatory framework had not been developed to address the distinctive needs of this new user group and there were implications for preparers of accounts, legislators and standard setters. A large part of this new user group considered itself neither wealthy nor sophisticated with regard to financial matters. Many new shareholders found themselves in receipt of an annual report for the first time. Two issues became clear fairly quickly: too many annual reports were being thrown away without being read, and too many shareholders who attempted to read the report were intimidated by the financial detail, confused by the terminology and only really comfortable with the chairman's statement and the other narrative sections at the front of the report. Companies were failing to communicate effectively with their new shareholders, and some were wasting substantial sums in printing and postage costs in the process.

1.2 Regulation

In response to representations from a variety of sources, including an initiative by the TSB Group plc (with over 2 million shareholders), the DTI consulted with the CBI, the Stock Exchange, the accountancy bodies and the Wider Share Ownership Council in 1987 and found that there was general support for a move to supply simpler, abbreviated information to shareholders who wished to receive it. The Government's drive to reduce the administrative burdens on businesses added further impetus to these changes. Some companies already produced two-part annual reports, one an annual review, the other containing the statutory information. Building societies had been required to produce a summary financial statement since 1986.

1.2.1 The Statutory Instruments

The Companies (Summary Financial Statement) Regulations 1990 (SI 1990 No 515) came into force on 1 April 1990 and were amended in 1992 in order to allow the holders of debenture stock to receive a summary financial statement, to implement the EC Bank Accounts

Directive, and to simplify the provisions relating to the consultation of new shareholders.[1]

The number of companies producing summary financial statements gradually increased, but rather more slowly than had been expected, for several reasons. One was the cumbersome administrative requirement for companies to send shareholders both the summary financial statement and the full annual accounts and directors' report in the first year, and a pre-paid card every year thereafter, in order to ensure that shareholders who wished to receive the full annual accounts and directors' report did so. Another was the inflexibility of the reporting requirements, a more important issue to those who were concerned with the value of the summary financial statement as a means of improving communications with shareholders. The summary profit and loss account and balance sheet had to follow the statutory order, and use the statutory headings. The technical, statutory headings in particular were seen as a bar to understanding. Last, but not least, the costs of setting up systems to administer the production and distribution of summary financial statements was a deterrent to many companies in the early 1990s.

The Companies (Summary Financial Statement) Regulations 1995 (SI 1995 No 2092) came into force on 1 September 1995. Apart from clarifying the requirements for banks and insurance companies, these Regulations gave companies the flexibility they had been asking for by removing the requirement for the statutory headings in the summary financial statement, although the requirement for the statutory order was retained. Companies have been slower to take advantage of this than might have been expected but several companies now make some attempt at explaining what some of the less familiar terms mean. The 1995 Regulations also simplified the consultation procedure required in the first year and permitted companies to write to shareholders, telling them what the summary financial statement would contain, rather than requiring them to

[1]   The Companies (Summary Financial Statement) Regulations 1992 (SI 1992 No 3075) and The Companies Act 1985 (Amendment of Sections 250 and 251) Regulations 1992 (SI 1992 No 3003).

send an example of the full annual accounts and directors' report, and the summary financial statement.

1.3 Current issues

1.3.1 The number of companies producing summary financial statements

The Merchant Handbook[2] lists the companies in the FTSE 250 issuing a summary financial statement in the years 1995 to 1998. There were 32 such companies in 1995, and 75 in 1998. This compares well with the mere handful that were issuing a summary financial statement in the early 1990s. As companies saw their competitors successfully issuing attractive summary financial statements (in contrast to long, dull and impenetrable annual reports), with real costs savings for some issuers in the medium term, the pressure increased for them to do likewise.

1.3.2 The cost issue

Some commentators consider that the primary motivation for the issue of summary financial statements by companies with large numbers of shareholders is to cut costs. Government has always admitted that cost is one of the reasons that companies are permitted to issue summary financial statements. *The Merchant Handbook 1998* notes that of FTSE 250 companies with over 110,000 shareholders, 80 per cent issued summary financial statements in 1998. Of companies with between 40,000 and 109,999 shareholders, 57 per cent issued summary financial statements, as did 11 per cent of those with under 40,000 shareholders. There is no hard evidence as to the numbers of shareholders required to make the issue of summary financial statements cost-effective, but our interviews with companies set out in Chapter 6 indicate that whilst some companies save money by issuing summary financial statements, some lose money and for others the exercise is cost neutral. Any savings that are likely to be made are by companies with a large number of

---

[2] *The Merchant Handbook 1998* (1998 Merchant Corporate Design).

shareholders, producing short summary financial statements, and in the medium rather than the short term.

Some companies then, continue to issue summary financial statements where it is clear in the short run, and likely in the long run, that it will result in increased costs, rather than cost savings. Such companies have other motives for the issue of summary financial statements.

1.3.3 The length and format of summary financial statements

A report published by the Institute of Chartered Accountants in England and Wales (ICAEW) in 1993[3] showed that of 20 companies issuing a summary financial statement at the time, the average length was 22 pages (the shortest being 12 pages and the longest being 32 pages). Another report by the same Institute published in 1996[4] showed that whereas in 1991 only one of 10 summary financial statements examined was 30 or more pages long, in 1993, five of the 10 were 30 or more pages long. The explanation given for this is the increase during that period of narrative on corporate governance and environmental disclosures. Only one of the 10 companies produced a cash flow statement in 1991, whereas over half of the more recent summary financial statements included cash flow information. Our survey of 20 companies set out in Chapter 4 shows that the average number of pages in current summary financial statements is 31 (the longest examined had 64 pages, the shortest had 13). Both of the reports noted above and our survey indicate that most companies use an A4 format.

The evidence shows that overall, summary financial statements are getting longer rather than shorter; however, this may be the effect of more companies producing a summary financial statement for the first time. In early years, there may be a temptation to include more

---

[3] *Evolution of Summary Financial Statements – Practical Experience to Date* (1993 ICAEW), see **2.3.2** below.
[4] *Summary Financial Statements – The Way Forward* (1996 ICAEW), see **2.5** below.

information, rather than less, for fear of omitting something that shareholders consider important. As companies gain experience and feedback from shareholders in this area, they are able to eliminate those sections that are of little value to shareholders – this has been the experience of the Rank Group (see Chapter 6).

Building society summary financial statements are shorter. This is partly because building societies did not have any experience of sending lengthy annual reports to their members, and partly as a result of the demutualisation of the large building societies with the resources to produce extensive reports. The societies that remain generally produce relatively short documents, of no more than four or five pages in many cases.

1.3.4 *The use of statutory headings*

Despite the 1995 changes to the Regulations that now permit the use of headings other than the statutory headings in the summary financial statement, few, if any companies have taken advantage of these provisions. The change was called for by companies and their auditors as a means of improving communications; it was given as one reason why more companies were not issuing financial statements when the DTI consulted on the issue in 1995. However, neither companies nor their auditors seem to be prepared to take the risk of establishing and using more user-friendly terminology. For companies the risk is of confusing shareholders; for auditors there are additional concerns about the consistency of summary financial statements produced with non-statutory headings, with the full annual accounts and directors' report. A few companies such as NatWest, BOC and Rank have started to include glossaries of financial terms in the summary financial statement.

1.3.5 *Effective communication*

It is argued that because over 90 per cent of shareholders of companies issuing summary financial statements are in receipt of them, summary financial statements are what shareholders want. The current Regulations permit companies a great degree of freedom in determining what is included and what is excluded from the summary financial statement. The companies included in our survey in Chapter 4 all included considerably more than was required by statute and previous surveys indicate that this has always been the case.

The basic requirement for a bare profit and loss account, balance sheet, summary directors' report and a single figure for directors' emoluments is inadequate as a means of effective communication. However, the quality of the additional information provided by companies has yet to be thoroughly analysed. With the exception of the ICAEW report detailed in **2.5** below, very little research has been conducted into the views of shareholders or their level of understanding. Effective communication is in any case difficult to measure, and questions remain as to whether shareholders really are better off with summary financial statements which provide substantial narrative but very little financial detail.

1.3.6 *Auditor involvement*

It is clear from our survey in Chapter 4 that the extent of auditor involvement varies from company to company. A few auditors include the entire document within the scope of their examination. Most confine their work to the financial statements. Some do, and some do not include the detailed information provided on directors' emoluments within the scope of their work (and the variation in detail provided in this area varies considerably from company to company).

1.3.7 *Interaction with preliminary announcements*

Some companies engineer the issue of the preliminary announcement and the summary financial statement to coincide. The survey in Chapter 4 indicates that 60 per cent of companies issue their summary financial statements within 60 days of the period-end and that the average delay between the period-end and the issue of the summary financial statement is 57 days. The issue of preliminary announcements follows a similar pattern. If companies can issue the summary financial statement and the preliminary announcement at more or less the same time, the question arises as to whether there is any need to issue two separate documents.

CHAPTER 2

The development of summary financial statements

2.1 The DTI consultation

As noted in Chapter 1 above, the DTI consulted with a variety of interested parties in 1987 and found that there was general support for a move to supply simpler, abbreviated information to shareholders who wished to receive it. The 1989 consultation paper[1] sought views on the mechanisms to be employed in ascertaining shareholders' wishes and minimum requirements as to the form and content of the summary financial statement.

2.1.1 Ascertaining shareholders' wishes

The mechanisms selected for ascertaining the wishes of shareholders later proved to be a barrier to the issue of summary financial statements and had to be changed. Two mechanisms were suggested and both involved shareholders receiving a pre-paid card each year asking them whether they wished to receive the full annual accounts and directors' report in that or future years. In the absence of a request for the full annual accounts and directors' report, a summary financial statement was to be sent. The main issue was one of timing; when should shareholders be asked? Before the circulation of the annual accounts and

---

[1] Consultative Document *Summary Financial Statements for Listed Public Companies* (1989 DTI).

directors' report, or at the same time? The two options were as follows:

(a) to send a summary financial statement only in the first year, together with the pre-paid reply card; or

(b) to canvass shareholders in advance.

There were disadvantages to both options. The first meant that those shareholders that wanted the full annual accounts and directors' report, particularly institutional shareholders, would have to take action in order to receive them and then wait for their delivery. The second would involve additional costs unless the requests were sent out, for example, with the interim report.

When the legislation was enacted the decision was taken to require companies to send both the full accounts and the summary financial statement in the first year, together with a pre-paid reply card indicating that the summary financial statement would be sent in future years unless the card was returned. This was in order to enable shareholders to make an informed decision but clearly involved substantial additional cost in the first year. This mechanism has been simplified by SI 1995 No 2092 which represents the current position (see **2.4** below).

2.1.2 The form and content of the summary financial statement

The consultation paper dealt with the derivation of the summary financial statement from the annual accounts and directors' report, statements as to the limitations of the summary financial statement, the auditors' statement, and presentation. The consultation paper envisaged the summary financial statement as a short document, similar to those produced by building societies, fitting easily onto two sides of A4. Example formats for the profit and loss account and balance sheet were given.

There appeared to be some flexibility in the consultation paper as to the formats required, but when the legislation was enacted, a requirement to use the statutory headings in the given order was introduced.

2.2 Support for summary financial statements

Coopers & Lybrand conducted a study in 1989, asking senior executives for their views on the possibility of issuing summary financial statements.[2] Over 80 per cent agreed that listed companies should be permitted to issue simplified accounts to shareholders (provided that full accounts were available as well), on the basis that it would be beneficial to smaller shareholders, recognising their different needs. Nearly 90 per cent believed it would relieve companies of unnecessary administrative burdens, although a significant number of the remaining 10 per cent believed that it would *increase* administrative burdens as a result of the need to prepare, print and distribute two reports. Eighty per cent of executives believed that there would be overall cost savings but in many cases it was expected that they would be marginal. Again, a significant minority believed that costs would increase. There was general agreement to the effect that companies with a large number of small shareholders would benefit most. Executives were less willing to commit themselves as to whether their companies would take advantage of any change in the law, but nearly all stated that any summary financial statement they produced would be in a glossy format, and a significant 40 per cent stated that they would no longer produce the full annual accounts and directors' report in a glossy format.

2.3 The first summary financial statements

Companies were first permitted to send their shareholders summary financial statements in 1990. A number of reports on progress in this area were produced over the next three years.

[2] *Summary Financial Statements. A Survey of Senior Businessmen's Views* (1989 Coopers & Lybrand). Forty-nine of Coopers & Lybrands' listed company clients responded to a questionnaire sent to all of their listed company clients.

2.3.1 ICAEW Research Board

The ICAEW Research Board published a paper in 1993 detailing the results of a questionnaire sent to 400 of the largest listed companies, including 50 financial companies.[3] The research was conducted in 1991 at which time the majority of respondents did not issue summary financial statements. The principal findings were as follows:

(a) *The number of summary financial statements issued*

Very few companies (11 of the 400 surveyed) had issued a summary financial statement. They included a few industrial companies (mostly the privatised utilities) and some financial institutions. One company had discontinued the production of summary financial statements and over 10 per cent had taken the decision not to issue summary financial statements, although a similar number were undecided. Those companies that did produce a summary financial statement were publishing more than the statutory minimum.

(b) *Costs*

For those companies that did produce a summary financial statement, cost savings were one of the main reasons for their issue but the additional administrative, production, printing and distribution costs meant that the exercise was not cost-effective for companies with few shareholders. A majority of companies believed that the issue of summary financial statements would result in increased costs.

(c) *Communications*

The perceived user group for summary financial statements included the general public, customers, potential shareholders, employees and consumer groups. For the full annual accounts and directors' report, the perceived user group was more likely to include financial analysts, lenders and bankers.

[3] Gray, S. J. and Roberts, C. B., *Summary Financial Statements* (1993 ICAEW Research Board).

The paper noted that whilst a third of companies believed that readership of the information would increase, only 21 per cent thought that shareholder understanding would be improved and most had doubts as to the real benefits to shareholders of summary information – nearly 30 per cent feared that shareholders might be misled. There was little support for the suggestion that summary financial statements would be of value to institutional investors or would improve the company's image in the financial markets. In many cases, the summary financial statements were in fact the full financial statements without the notes, but no attempt had been made to render the technical information therein more relevant to users.

(d) *Format and content*

The paper noted that a majority of companies issued two related documents: the annual review containing the summary financial statement, and the annual accounts containing the statutory information. Shareholders wanting full annual accounts received both documents; those not requiring the full financial statements received only the annual review, although some companies sent both to all shareholders. Even then, most companies disclosed more than the statutory minimum and included information such as segmental information, a financial calendar and dividend information.

2.3.2 ICAEW Financial Reporting Committee research

The ICAEW issued a further paper in 1993 entitled *Evolution of Summary Financial Statements – Practical Experience to Date*, involving a questionnaire sent in the summer of 1992 to 20 companies known to have issued a summary financial statement. There were 14 respondents. This research differed from the previous survey to the extent that it was conducted at a later date, when reporting practice had had some chance to develop, and all of the respondents had experience in the issue of a summary financial statement. The findings were as follows:

(a) *Costs*

Some companies reported no savings, others reported savings of up to 33 per cent. The paper noted that first year costs are likely to be heavier, and that it is unhelpful to take a short-term view of costs as any savings are likely to be made in subsequent years in the form of a reduction in administration, printing and postage costs.

(b) *Administrative issues*

The paper noted the requirement to use the headings and the order prescribed by the statutory instrument. It suggested that communications would be improved if companies were permitted to use alternative wording, as most shareholders would be more concerned with understanding the summary financial statement than with making inter-company comparisons. A safeguard already existed in the form of the requirement for auditors to make a statement as to the consistency of the summary financial statement with the full annual accounts and directors' report.

As in previous surveys, the majority of respondents issued two-part annual accounts, one being the annual review and summary financial statement, the other being the statutory information. The directors' report sometimes appeared in one, sometimes in the other.

(c) *Content*

The main areas in which companies were providing significant additional information beyond that required by statute included matters relating to directors (their biographies, emoluments and shareholdings), political and charitable contributions, segmental information and cash flows.

The average length of the summary financial statement was four pages and all but one summary financial statement was in A4 format.

The paper made two important points. Firstly, the fact that shareholders prefer to read a summary rather than the full annual accounts and directors' report does not of itself prove that communications have improved; nevertheless, the *perception* on the part of shareholders of improved communications is valuable in itself, and it is better that something is read (i.e., the summary financial statement), rather than nothing. Secondly, the fact that the legislation relies on inertia (sending back the pre-paid card) means that conclusions as to shareholders' real wishes must be drawn with care. However, the paper noted an interesting initiative by Reckitt & Colman who ascertained shareholders' wishes by writing to them asking if they wished to receive a summary financial statement, in addition to the method prescribed by legislation for ascertaining shareholders' wishes. Twenty-seven per cent of all shareholders responded indicating that they did wish to receive summary financial statements, rather than the full annual accounts and directors' report. On the other hand, the fact that over 90 per cent of BICC's shareholders were apparently willing to receive a summary financial statement was no bar to the company discontinuing their production on the grounds of costs and complexity.

2.4   The 1995 amendments

2.4.1   The Companies (Summary Financial Statement) Regulations 1995

The Companies (Summary Financial Statement) Regulations 1995 (SI 1995 No 2092) are the Regulations now in force. They are set out in detail in Chapter 3 and Appendix 1.

The DTI in its consultation was concerned about the relatively small number of companies that were issuing a summary financial statement (approximately 30 at the time). The One Hundred Group of Finance Directors and others had indicated that there were three issues:

(a)   the Regulations were poorly laid out and difficult to follow;

(b) the procedures for consulting shareholders were cumbersome and expensive;

(c) the requirement to use the statutory order and headings in the summary financial statement was unnecessary and did not facilitate effective communication with private shareholders.

Two main changes were made to the Regulations. The previous Regulations (SI 1992 No 3075) had required companies to send shareholders both the full annual accounts and directors' report, and a summary financial statement. The requirement was not dropped, but an alternative mechanism was introduced whereby the company could write to shareholders describing the content of the summary financial statement and informing them that the summary financial statement would be sent unless they indicated on the pre-paid reply card that they wished to receive the full annual accounts and directors' report. Companies were also permitted to make a clear statement as to where and how a copy of the full annual accounts and directors' report could be obtained, instead of sending a pre-paid reply card with the summary financial statement every year.

The second main change related to the form and content of the summary financial statement. The previous Regulations had required the summary financial statement to use the prescribed headings as well as the prescribed order. The current Regulations permit companies to use such headings as they see fit, albeit in the prescribed order.

The Regulations also aligned the requirements for insurance companies with the requirements of the EU Insurance Accounts Directive.

The DTI had made a variety of suggestions. It had sought views as to whether, for example:

(a) the statement informing shareholders that they would receive a summary financial statement rather than the full annual accounts and directors' report should contain a warning that the summary financial statement was not a substitute for the full annual accounts and directors' report, and make some reference to the audit of the full annual accounts;

(b) companies should be required to pay for the postage on pre-paid cards sent to overseas shareholders;

(c) the requirement to maintain the statutory order for the profit and loss account and balance sheet should be dropped, as well as the requirement to use the statutory headings.

Suggestions (a) and (c) were dropped. With regard to (b), it was decided that companies should not be required to send pre-paid cards to shareholders outside the European Economic Area (EEA).

2.5   Summary Financial Statements – The Way Forward (1996 ICAEW)

2.5.1   Developments in reporting practice

This paper sought to demonstrate the effectiveness of summary financial statements as a means of communication, and emphasised the need for quality information for shareholders, rather than quantity, which sometimes served to obscure important messages.

2.5.2   Shareholder survey

The shareholder survey[4] involved a questionnaire sent to substantial numbers of shareholders of three large companies, with over 1,500 respondents. The results were as might be expected: shareholders preferred a short document to a longer one, were much more likely to read the narrative sections than the financial sections, and they concentrated on financial highlights, rather than the financial statements. Whilst most shareholders read at least parts of the

---

[4]   Based on an unpublished 1995 survey by A. Hansford and R. Hussey of the Bristol Business School.

annual review, and many retained the document for a period of some months, many also had difficulties in understanding the financial statements.

2.5.3 Case histories – three companies

The survey also gave details of three companies' experiences of introducing summary financial statements (British American Tobacco (BAT), Pilkington and Smith & Nephew).

BAT had been issuing two free-standing reports until 1991, when as a result of research conducted on its behalf by MORI showing that the chairman's statement and the financial highlights were the most widely-read parts of the annual report, the decision was taken to produce a single two-part report and accounts, which was sent to all shareholders. A summary financial statement, together with the director's report and accounts, formed the full annual report. Private shareholders could easily identify the summary financial statements directed at them. Information beyond the statutory minimum in the summary financial statement included summary segmental data and a corporate governance report. This model is used by several organisations, but it does involve an element of duplication and decisions almost every year as to where to accommodate new disclosures required by changes in legislation, the Listing Rules, accounting standards and best practice. BAT considered there were many benefits to the issue of summary financial statements. Over 90 per cent of shareholders were in receipt of the summary financial statement, which because of its comparative length, was quicker (and cheaper) to print. Because of this, the company decided that it was no longer necessary to send the preliminary announcement to shareholders, as the summary financial statement had effectively replaced it. Costs had risen in the first year, but they fell in subsequent years. BAT had over 1.5 million shareholders at the time. More significantly perhaps, the company conducted research into private shareholders' views after the summary financial statements had been sent, which showed a clear improvement in the shareholders' perception of their own understanding.

Pilkington noted hostility amongst analysts to a similar two-part format to the annual report, the substantial management time required to ensure the consistency of the two documents, the administrative effort of ensuring that shareholders received the correct document, and the likelihood that the summary financial statement would increase in length over time. Nevertheless, savings were achieved on a shareholder base of 37,000.

Smith & Nephew had a similar number of shareholders over 95 per cent of whom were in receipt of the summary financial statement which doubled as a corporate brochure and was distributed internally as well as externally. The company eventually took a slightly different approach to the production of the summary financial statement. One full annual report was produced, but at the binding stage, the statement of total recognised gains and losses, the movement in shareholders' funds, the parent company balance sheet and the notes were removed from the summary financial statement. Despite difficulties with summary financial statements, the company continued with their issue on the grounds that modern accounting disclosures actively militated against clarity of communication for the private shareholder.

2.6   Shareholders' views

There is a trend in corporate reporting to attempt to establish the needs of users of corporate reports by communicating directly with them, rather than by making assumptions about them. The surveys noted above concentrated on the experience of companies in the production of summary financial statements. Some companies made efforts to obtain feedback from private investors, but the first published survey focusing on the views of shareholders was produced in September 1996 by Deloitte & Touche.

2.6.1 *Shareholder survey by Deloitte & Touche*

The authors of Deloitte & Touche's Corporate Communication *Shareholders' Views of the Annual Review*[5] worked closely with two companies, Arjo Wiggins Appleton and BAA, and their shareholders. A questionnaire was sent to 4,000 shareholders in total and just over 1,000 replies were received. Shareholders stated that the primary functions of the annual review were to assess the performance of the company and to keep abreast of developments. Less than 30 per cent (for both companies) said that they used it to aid investment decisions and about 35 per cent (on average) said that other information would be required for investment decisions. A high proportion of shareholders in both companies (around 70 per cent) were aware that they could request the full annual report. The chairman's statement was the document most likely to be read, the chief executive's review and the directors' emoluments came a roughly equal second. Less than 20 per cent of both groups read the balance sheet, the directors' report, the cash flow statement or the auditors' statement. Several conclusions were drawn: the statutory information was the least read and the least useful to shareholders. Shareholders were only prepared to spend a limited amount of time on the document and the shorter the document, the more likely it was to be read.

Shareholders were also asked about their understanding of the annual review. Between 30 per cent and 40 per cent of shareholders in both companies considered their general level of understanding to be 'good or very good'. Around 50 per cent for both companies considered it 'adequate' and less than five per cent considered it 'poor'. Shareholders were asked about their understanding of the various sections of the report; under 50 per cent for both companies found the statutory information 'easy' to understand. An interesting question relating to how long shareholders kept the document before throwing it away showed that a quarter kept it for a year. The conclusion drawn from this

[5] Hansford, A., Hussey, J. and Hussey, R. *Corporate Communication. Shareholders' Views of the Annual Review* (1996 Deloitte & Touche).

information was expressed in terms of the value of the report to shareholders (although it is tempting to think that it might have something to do with the individual's attitude towards the retention of bits of paper generally). Relatively few shareholders in either company felt that any section contained too much or too little information.

The results of this survey are of course likely to be skewed in favour of the financially 'active'; BAA's shareholder respondents in particular contained a high level of those categorising themselves as professional/technical/managerial. The level of understanding of the majority (the 75 per cent that did not reply) remains unclear.

CHAPTER 3

Regulation

3.1 General

The main regulation relating to summary financial statements is s251 of the Companies Act 1985. This deals with the basic conditions that are required of listed companies wishing to send a summary financial statement to their members and others. The Companies (Summary Financial Statement) Regulations 1995 (SI 1995 No 2092) and the schedules thereto deal in greater detail with the conditions for sending summary financial statements, the manner in which the wishes of entitled persons are to be ascertained, and the form and content of the summary financial statement. Separate schedules for banking and insurance companies and groups are included. The Companies (Revision of Defective Accounts and Report) Regulations 1990 (SI 1990 No 2750) deal with procedures to be applied where defective financial statements (financial statements not prepared in accordance with the Companies Act 1985) have been issued. The sections and regulations applicable to non banking/insurance companies are reproduced in Appendix 1.

3.1.1 Non-statutory guidance

There is no guidance issued by the Accounting Standards Board (ASB) specifically devoted to the summary financial statement, however, the Auditing Practices Board (APB) adopted an Auditing Guideline from its predecessor, the Auditing Practices Committee (APC), Auditing Guideline 506 *The Auditors' Statement on the Summary Financial Statement* (AG 506). This guidance was originally issued in May 1991 but is still relevant, except to the extent that the wording of the auditors' report has been superseded. Auditing Guideline 506 is reproduced in Appendix 2.

Regulation relating to building societies is dealt with in **3.7** below.

3.2 Companies Act 1985

The original legislation introduced by the Companies Act 1989 was effective as of 1 March 1990. The current position is as follows.

3.2.1 Basic requirements

Section 251 sets out which companies are entitled to issue a summary financial statement, under what conditions they are permitted to do so, and the requirement for the involvement of auditors. Section 251 applies to public companies listed on the London and Irish Stock Exchanges. Such companies need not send copies of the annual accounts, directors' and auditors' reports required under s238 to shareholders, debenture holders and others (entitled persons); they may instead send them a summary financial statement. However, entitled persons are entitled to receive the annual accounts and directors' report if they so wish and SI 1995 No 2092 sets out the manner in which companies are required to ascertain their wishes (see **3.3** below).

3.2.2 Directors' and auditors' statements

A summary financial statement is required to contain statements by directors and auditors. It must state that it is only a summary of information in the annual accounts and directors' report. The auditors must give two opinions, firstly as to whether the summary financial statement is consistent with the annual accounts and directors' report and secondly, whether it complies with the Regulations. The auditors must also state whether or not the auditors' report on the annual accounts was qualified or made any statement 'by exception' as to the lack of proper accounting records or the failure to obtain necessary information and explanations. If there was any qualification, or any statement, it is in effect necessary to reproduce the audit report in full, and include the substance of notes that may be referred to in the report (i.e., 'any further material needed to understand the qualification').

It is unusual for the type of company that regularly issues a summary financial statement to receive a qualified audit report. Nevertheless, the most common type of audit qualification relates to a limitation in the scope of the auditors' work and where such reports are issued, it is common for statements on accounting records or information and explanations to be made, the lack of them usually being the cause of the scope limitation.

3.2.3 Non-statutory accounts

Section 240 deals with the publication of statutory and non-statutory accounts. It requires non-statutory accounts to carry a statement to the effect that they are non-statutory accounts, to state whether statutory accounts have been filed with the registrar for the relevant period and to make certain references to the auditors' reports. These provisions would apply to summary financial statements were they not exempted from them by s251(7).

3.3 SI 1995 No 2092 – administrative matters

This Statutory Instrument fleshes out the basic requirements of s251 Companies Act 1985. It deals with conditions for sending out summary financial statements, their form and content, and was effective as of 1 September 1995.

3.3.1 Conditions for sending out a summary financial statement

Listed companies may not send out a summary financial statement if they are prohibited from doing so by their own memorandum or articles of association or by any agreement with debenture holders.

This provision applies equally where the constitution or agreement requires the sending of full annual accounts and directors' report, or prohibits the sending of a summary financial statement. This will normally be a minor issue for a large company. The summary financial statement must be approved by the board of directors, signed on the board's behalf by a board member, and sent out within the period allowed for the delivery of full accounts under s244 Companies Act 1985 (i.e., seven months for a public company).

3.3.2   Ascertaining the recipients' wishes

Companies must establish that entitled persons do not wish to receive the full annual accounts and directors' report before they are permitted to send a summary financial statement. Either the entitled person:

(a)   notifies the company in writing to that effect; or

(b)   fails to respond to a notification informing him that he will in future receive a summary financial statement unless he fills in and returns a pre-paid reply card, indicating his wish to receive full annual accounts and directors' report (by ticking a box); or

(c)   fails to respond to a notification similar to that described in (b) above, sent with a copy of both the full annual accounts and directors' report and the summary financial statement.

The options under (b) and (c) above are known as 'consultation by notice' and 'relevant consultation'. Option (a) is clearly rarely used by shareholders, and the notification must be received by the company at least 28 days before the annual accounts and directors' report is sent out.

3.3.3   Consultation by notice

The notification sent to shareholders must give a description of the summary financial statement, together with a prominent statement to the effect that the summary financial statement will not contain sufficient information to allow for as full an understanding of the financial position as would be provided by the annual accounts and directors' report. There must also be reference to the report to be made by the auditors and the fact that the full annual accounts and directors' report will be available, free of charge. Prepayment on the card is not required for entitled persons that are not registered at an EEA address. The card must be sent at least 28 days before the annual accounts and directors' report are due to be sent out and the entitled person must be given at least 21 days to come to a decision.

3.3.4   Relevant consultation

In these circumstances the entitled person has an example of the difference between the annual accounts and directors' report and the summary financial statement in front of him; the prominent statements as to the nature of the summary financial statement are not therefore required.

For all three methods of notification, the notification or deemed notification stands until revoked by the entitled person.

3.4   Form and content

Part III of SI 1995 No 2092 and the Schedules thereto deal with the form and content of summary financial statements. Summary financial statements must state the name of the person who signed them on behalf of the board. They must contain a statement in a prominent position indicating that the summary financial statement does not allow for a full understanding of the financial position and that the full annual accounts and directors' report must be consulted for those purposes. It must state that the full annual accounts and directors' report are available free of charge, and set out where and how they may be obtained, as well as indicating that recipients may elect in writing to receive full annual accounts and directors' reports for all future years.

3.4.1 Form and content

The Schedules to SI 1995 No 2092 set out the requirements in respect of companies and groups, including banking and insurance companies and groups. The requirements for a non-banking/insurance group from Schedule 1 are set out below.

The order for the content of summary financial statements is prescribed, the headings are not. Companies must include any 'other' information necessary to ensure that the summary financial statement is consistent with the full annual accounts and directors' report.

The *summary directors' report* must be derived from the full directors' report and include the following:

(a) a business review;

(b) the proposed dividend if this does not appear in the summary profit and loss account;

(c) significant post-balance sheet events; and

(d) likely future developments.

The summary financial statement must also contain a list of directors. Sometimes this information is included in the full annual accounts and directors' report and the summary financial statement is cross-referenced to them; sometimes the opposite is true (particularly where two-part reports are issued), but in both cases, this applies only where all shareholders receive the full statutory as well as summary information.

The *summary profit and loss account* must be derived from the full profit and loss account and include the following:

(a) turnover;

(b) income from interests in associated undertakings;

(c) net interest and similar items receivable/payable;

(d) profit before tax;

(e) tax;

(f) profit after tax;

(g) minority interests;

(h) extraordinary items after tax;

(i) profit or loss for the year; and

(j) dividends paid (and proposed, if not included in the summary directors' report).

The summary financial statement must also disclose a single, aggregate figure for directors' emoluments. This contrasts with the substantial information on directors' emoluments actually provided by many companies. Again, the information in practice is sometimes cross-referenced between the summary financial statement and the full annual accounts and directors' report.

The Stock Exchange Listing Rules require that an earnings per share figure be included in summary financial statements (Chapter 12.54).

The *summary balance sheet* must be derived from the full balance sheet and include all headings which are assigned a letter (rather than a number) in the relevant statutory format. This means that for a non-banking/insurance group, the balance sheet is likely to include the following:

(a) fixed assets;

(b) current assets;

(c) cash at bank and in hand;

(d) creditors: amounts falling due within one year;

(e) net current assets/liabilities;

(f) total assets less current liabilities;

(g) creditors: amounts falling due after one year;

(h)   provisions for liabilities and charges;

(i)   minority interests; and

(j)   capital and reserves.

This format is Format 1, taken from Part 1 Sch 4 Companies Act 1985. Three other items are assigned letters in this format: called up share capital not paid; prepayments and accrued income, and accruals and deferred income. Companies are permitted to and normally do include these items under alternative numbered headings and they have therefore been omitted. 'Minority interests' may alternatively be included after capital and reserves.

Corresponding amounts must be included for both summary profit and loss account and balance sheet, after any adjustments to ensure comparability with the current year. Frequent changes in accounting standards over the past few years have meant that such adjustments are often required.

3.5   *The Companies (Revision of Defective Accounts and Report) Regulations 1990*

The Companies (Revision of Defective Accounts and Report) Regulations 1990 (SI 1990 No 2750) are not often used as relatively few companies, either voluntarily, or at the behest of the Financial Reporting Review Panel (FRRP), go through the formality and expense of revising defective accounts; there are other means of dealing with defective financial statements (usually a correction in the subsequent financial statements).

Section 14 of SI 1990 No 2750 requires that where a summary financial statement would not comply with the requirements of s251 Companies Act 1985, if it had been prepared by reference to the revised annual accounts or directors' report, the directors must send a revised summary financial statement to any person in receipt of the original summary financial statement and certain others. This deals with the situation in which the accounts and directors' report are revised to the extent that the original summary financial statement is no longer consistent with them. It is not necessary to send out a revised summary financial statement where the revisions to the annual accounts or directors' report have no effect on the summary financial statement's consistency with them; in such circumstances, the directors inform those in receipt of the summary financial statement that the accounts and report from which the summary financial statement was derived have been revised, and that the revision has no bearing on the summary financial statement.

3.6 *Auditing guidance*

There are three sources of current auditing guidance issued by the Auditing Practices Board (APB):

(a) Auditing Guideline 506 *The Auditors' Statement on the Summary Financial Statement* (1991);

(b) SAS 600 *Auditors' Reports on Financial Statements* (1993); and

(c) Practice Note 8 *Reports by Auditors Under Company Legislation in the United Kingdom* (1994).

The Auditing Guideline contains the substance of guidance for auditors, the other two sources merely contain example auditors' statements.

3.6.1 *Auditing Guideline 506 – basic requirements*

This guidance was based on regulations which have been replaced; however, the requirement for auditors to make a statement on (a) and (b) below, and for statements (c) and (d) to be made have not changed and the guidance is therefore relevant. Auditors are required under s251 Companies Act 1985 to report on:

(a) the consistency of the summary financial statement with the full annual accounts and directors' report; and

(b) the compliance of the summary financial statement with s251 Companies Act 1985 and the Regulations made thereunder.

These requirements are interdependent. The Regulations SI 1990 No 2750 require that the summary financial statement is consistent with the annual accounts and directors' report. Therefore, if the summary financial statement is not consistent, it cannot comply with the Regulations. The Regulations also require that the summary financial statement be 'derived' from the full annual accounts and directors' report. Situations could arise in which information is included in the summary financial statement which is not inconsistent with the full annual accounts and directors' report, but which is not properly derived from them (i.e., extraneous material).

Section 251 Companies Act 1985 also requires there to be within the summary financial statement a statement as to whether:

(c) the auditors' report on the full annual accounts was qualified, and if so, to set out the report together with any further material needed to understand the qualification (such as a note to which the qualification refers); and

(d) the auditors' report contained any statement 'by exception' under s237(2) or 237(3) on the maintenance of proper accounting records, the agreement of the accounts with the underlying records, the adequacy of returns, and any failure to obtain information or explanations.

The legislation states that the statement should be made in the summary financial statement. It does not stipulate who should make the statement and, in practice, it is sometimes made by auditors and sometimes by directors.

Few, if any, companies issuing summary financial statements refer either to an inconsistency with the full annual accounts and directors' report, or to non-compliance with the Regulations, or to a qualified audit report, or to any of the statements 'by exception'. Most auditors will therefore have little experience in dealing with inconsistencies that cannot be resolved by discussion with directors.

References in auditors' reports (on full annual accounts) to fundamental inherent uncertainties (such as litigation or the going concern status of an entity) under SAS 600 *Auditors' Reports on Financial Statements* are not qualifications. They are not therefore caught under the requirement for the reproduction of the audit report in the summary financial statements. Nevertheless, it seems highly likely in most cases that in order to achieve consistency with the full annual accounts and directors' report, some reference must be made to the uncertainty both in the summary financial statement itself, as well as in the auditors' statement (see **3.6.4** below).

3.6.2 *The auditors' procedures*

Auditors should establish at the planning stage of the audit whether or not a summary financial statement is to be produced and plan to conduct their work on the summary financial statement in parallel with the work on the full annual accounts and directors' report, in order to give their opinion on the two documents at the same time. The engagement letter should refer to the respective responsibilities of directors and auditors in relation to the summary financial statement.

The guidance sets out examples of the type of inconsistency that may arise:

(a) inaccurate extraction of information from the accounts and directors' report (e.g., incorrect classification of balance sheet items);

(b) summarisation in an inconsistent manner (e.g., unduly selective summarisation of the directors' report);

(c) omission of information which is not required by the Regulations but which is required to achieve consistency (e.g., information relating to exceptional items or subsequent events which auditors consider fundamental to shareholders' understanding).

Such inconsistencies should be discussed with directors and eliminated. If consistency is not achieved, the auditors' qualify their statement and include a description of the inconsistency.

3.6.3 *Other information issued with summary financial statements*

Most, if not all, summary financial statements are issued as part of a larger document including information which is not required by the legislation, such as a chairman's statement. In practice, auditors include non-statutory financial information (such as cash flow statements) within the scope of their examination, and exclude non-financial information (such as the chairman's statement). The auditing guidance requires that the summary financial statement should be clearly identified and not associated with any information that could be misleading. Auditors 'urge' directors not to issue documents containing the summary financial statement until they have had a chance to read them and if they disagree with any of them, they should take legal advice. In practice, auditors make it a condition of their agreement to report on the summary financial statement that they have sight of the other information well in advance of publication.

3.6.4 *Auditors' statements*

The auditors' statement set out in the Appendix to the Auditing Guideline consists of a single opinion paragraph on the consistency of the summary financial statement with the annual accounts and directors' report and its compliance with s251 Companies Act 1985 and the Regulations. The wording of this statement is set out in Appendix 2 to this book but is no longer used in practice, as it has been superseded.

SAS 600 *Auditors' Reports on Financial Statements* was issued in May 1993. In the *Note on Legal Requirements Applicable to Companies*, reference is made to the Auditing Guideline. Two points are made. The first is that the wording of Example 6 of Appendix 2 to the SAS supersedes the example given in the Auditing Guideline. The second is that where it is 'considered appropriate', the auditors should make reference to fundamental uncertainties in their statement. The wording of Example 6 in Appendix 2 to SAS 600 is as follows:

AUDITORS' STATEMENT TO THE SHAREHOLDERS OF XYZ PLC

We have audited the summary financial statement set out above/on page . . .

Respective responsibilities of directors and auditors

The summary financial statement is the responsibility of the directors. Our responsibility is to report to you our opinion as to whether the statement is consistent with the full financial statements and directors' report.

Basis of opinion

We conducted our audit in accordance with Auditing Standards issued by the Auditing Practices Board. The audit of a summary financial statement comprises an assessment of whether the statement contains all information necessary to ensure consistency with the full financial statements and directors' report and of whether the detailed information required by law has been properly extracted from those documents and included in the summary statement.

Our report on the company's full financial statements includes information on the responsibilities of directors and auditors relating to the preparation and audit of financial statements and on the basis of our opinion on the financial statements.

Opinion

In our opinion the summary financial statement above/on page . . . is consistent with the full financial statements and directors' report of XYZ plc for the year ended . . . and complies with the requirements of the Companies Act 1985, and regulations made thereunder, applicable to summary financial statements.

Registered auditors
Date

Address

Example paragraphs for inclusion in the basis of opinion section where applicable:

(1) *Referring to a fundamental uncertainty:*
    Our report on the group's full financial statements included an explanatory paragraph concerning a fundamental uncertainty arising from the outcome of possible litigation against B Ltd, a subsidiary undertaking of the company, for an alleged breach of environmental regulations. Details of the circumstances relating to this fundamental uncertainty are described in note . . . of the summary financial statement. Our opinion on the full financial statements is not qualified in this respect.

(2) *Referring to a qualified opinion:*
    Our opinion on the company's full financial statements was qualified as a result of a disagreement with the accounting treatment of the company's leased assets. Details of the circumstances giving rise to that opinion are set out in note . . . of the summary financial statement.

Auditing Standards within SAS 600 are mandatory, unlike Auditing Guidelines or the Practice Notes. However, the Appendices to SAS 600 are not mandatory and most auditors do not use the wording suggested by SAS 600; in particular, they do not state that the auditors have *audited* the summary financial statement.

Practice Note 8 *Reports by Auditors Under Company Legislation in the United Kingdom* (PN 8) was issued in 1994. Practice Notes are persuasive rather than prescriptive, they are indicative of good practice and have similar status to the explanatory material in Auditing Standards. Example 5 of Appendix 1 to PN 8 is the most closely followed in practice and reads as follows:

AUDITORS' STATEMENT TO THE SHAREHOLDERS OF XYZ PLC

We have examined the summary financial statement set out above/ on page . . .

Respective responsibilities of directors and auditors

The summary financial statement is the responsibility of the directors. Our responsibility is to report to you our opinion on its preparation and consistency with the full financial statements and directors' report.

Basis of opinion

We conducted our work in accordance with Auditing Guideline 'The auditor's statement on the summary financial statement' adopted by the Auditing Practices Board.

Opinion

In our opinion the summary financial statement is consistent with the full financial statements and directors' report of XYZ plc for the year ended . . . and complies with the requirements of the Companies Act 1985, and regulations made thereunder, applicable to summary financial statements.

Registered auditors   *Address*
Date

Several detailed comments are made in PN 8: in the absence of any other requirements the auditors' statement may be made to shareholders; references to fundamental uncertainties in the audit report on the full annual accounts are also made in the auditors' statement and the statement is dated as soon as possible after the date on which the audit report on the full annual accounts is dated (but not before the directors have approved the summary financial statement).

3.6.5 US, Canadian and Australian requirements

Securities and Exchange Commission (SEC) listed companies in the US are not permitted to send their stockholders summary financial statements instead of full financial statements. The SEC consulted some years ago on the possibility of permitting listed companies to send their private shareholders abbreviated financial statements but no agreement could be reached as to the content of such financial statements and the proposals were dropped. Nevertheless, many companies send their stockholders *condensed* financial information as well as the full information. Auditors of listed US companies are required to make a statement on four matters when their clients produce condensed financial information:

(a) that the auditor has audited and expressed an opinion on the complete financial statements;

(b) the date of the auditor's report on the complete financial statements;

(c) the type of opinion expressed; and

(d) whether the information is fairly stated in all material respects in relation to the complete financial statements from which it is derived.

The auditor's opinion is as follows:

INDEPENDENT AUDITOR'S REPORT

'We have audited, in accordance with generally accepted auditing standards, the consolidated balance sheet of X company and subsidiaries as of December 31 19X0, and the related consolidated statements of income, retained earnings and cash flows for the year then ended (not presented herein); and in our report dated February 15, 19X1, we expressed an unqualified opinion on those consolidated financial statements.

In our opinion, the information set forth in the accompanying condensed consolidated financial statements is fairly stated, in all material respects, in relation to the consolidated financial statements from which it has been derived.'

These statements are not required if the condensed financial statements are included in a document that contains the full audited financial statements.

The auditors' report on summarised financial statements in Canada states that they 'fairly summarize, in all material respects, the related complete financial statements . . .'. A warning to the effect that the summarized financial statements do not contain all the disclosures required by GAAP, and that the full financial statements should be consulted, also appears in the auditors' report.

Some Australian companies are permitted to prepare 'concise financial reports' in the place of full financial reports. The auditors' report on these reports is a full audit report and states that the financial report complies with the relevant accounting standard.

3.7 Building societies

Building societies have been required to send their members and depositors a summary financial statement since 1986 and the provisions are very similar to those required of companies. Less than 70 building societies remain in existence.

The Building Societies Act 1986 was amended by the Building Societies Act 1997 which made fairly minor changes to bring the Act up to date. The Building Societies (Accounts and Related Provisions) Regulations 1998 (SI 1998 No 504) give the detailed requirements as to the content of the summary financial statement. The relevant sections of this legislation are reproduced in Appendix 1.

3.7.1 Section 76 Building Societies Act 1986

Section 76 of the Building Societies Act 1986 requires that the directors of building societies prepare for members and depositors a summary financial statement derived from the annual accounts, annual business statement and directors' report. The business statement is a statement of financial ratios together with an explanation of movements therein. The summary financial statement must contain similar statements to those required of companies, i.e., that:

(a) it is only a summary of information in the accounts, business statement and directors' report;

(b) the accounts have been audited (in so far as they have been);

(c) the accounts, business statement and directors' report will be available to members and depositors free of charge at every office of the society after a specified date.

The summary financial statement must include an auditors' statement as to his opinion on the *consistency* of the summary financial statement with the accounts, business statement and directors' report and on its *conformity* with the section and relevant regulations. Summary financial statements must be signed by two directors (on behalf of the board) and the chief executive. They must be sent to members no later than 21 days before the AGM, together with a copy of the auditors' report on the full annual accounts if it was qualified.

3.7.2   SI 1998 No 504

Section 10 of this Statutory Instrument details the content of summary financial statements and requires that they comprise:

(a) the statutory statements required by s76 Building Societies Act 1986;

(b) a summary directors' report;

(c) a summary statement (profit and loss account); and

(d) a summary of key financial ratios (business statement);

all in accordance with Sch 10 to the Regulations. There is no prohibition on the inclusion of additional material.

3.7.3 *Schedule 10 to SI 1998 No 504*

Schedule 10 requires the following formats.

FORMAT OF SUMMARY STATEMENT

Results for the year	*This year* £	*Last year* £
1. Net interest receivable	•	•
2. Other income and charges	•	•
3. Administrative expenses	•	•
4. Provisions	•	•
5. Profit/Loss [NOTE 1] for the year before taxation	•	•
6. Taxation	•	•
7. Minority interest [NOTE 2]	•	•
8. Extraordinary income and charges after tax	•	•
9. Profit/Loss [NOTE 1] for the year	•	•

Financial position at end of year

Assets

10. Liquid assets	•	•
11. Mortgages	•	•
12. Other loans	•	•
13. Fixed and other assets	•	•
14. Total assets	•	•

Liabilities

15. Shares	•	•
16. Borrowings	•	•
17. Other liabilities	•	•
18. Subordinated liabilities	•	•
19. Subscribed capital	•	•
20. Reserves	•	•
21. Other capital [NOTE 3]	•	•
22. Total liabilities	•	•

NOTE 1: Delete as appropriate.
NOTE 2: Group accounts society only.
NOTE 3: The heading may be replaced by 'Revaluation reserve' where this is the only category of 'Other capital' in the balance sheet in the annual accounts.

FORMAT OF SUMMARY OF KEY FINANCIAL RATIOS

	This year %	*Last year* %
1. Gross capital as a percentage of shares and borrowings.	•	•
2. Liquid assets as a percentage of shares and borrowings.	•	•
3. Profit/Loss [NOTE 1] for the year as a percentage of mean total assets.	•	•
4. Management expenses as a percentage of mean total assets.	•	•

NOTE 1: Delete as appropriate.

An explanation of the key financial ratios is required; there is no requirement to use the terms 'This Year' and 'Last Year'.

The summary directors' report includes the following summary reviews:

(a) of business during the year and the financial position at the end of it;

(b) of important events affecting the society during the year;

(c) of important post balance sheet events;

(d) of likely future developments.

3.7.4   *Audit requirements*

Practice Note 18 *The Audit of Building Societies in the United Kingdom* issued by the Auditing Practices Board deals with the audit of building societies generally. It gives an example auditors' statement which is based on PN 8 and reads as follows:

AUDITORS' STATEMENT ON THE SUMMARY FINANCIAL STATEMENT

Auditors' statement to the members and depositors of [   ] Building Society

We have examined the summary financial statement set out [above] [on pages x to x].

Respective responsibilities of directors and auditors

The summary financial statement is the responsibility of the directors. Our responsibility is to report to you our opinion on its consistency with the full financial statements [annual accounts], annual business statement and directors' report and its conformity with the requirements of Section 76 of the Building Societies Act 1986 and regulations made under it.

Basis of opinion

We conducted our examination of the statement in accordance with the Auditing Guideline 'The auditors' statement on the summary financial statement' adopted by the Auditing Practices Board.

Opinion

In our opinion the summary financial statement is consistent with the full financial statements [annual accounts], the annual business statement and directors' report of [   ] Building Society for the year ended [   ] and conforms with the requirements of Section 76 of the Building Societies Act 1986, and regulations made under it.

Registered auditors   *Address*
Date

There is no specific auditing guidance directed at building societies and the APC Auditing Guideline detailed in **3.6** above is therefore relevant.

CHAPTER 4

Survey: 20 summary financial statements

4.1 Summary financial statements included

The summary financial statements of the following FTSE 100 companies were included in the survey:

BAT	BOC	BP Amoco
British Telecom	Cadbury Schweppes	Glaxo-Wellcome
Lloyds TSB	NatWest	National Grid
National Power	Orange	Pearson
Pilkington	Rank	Reckitt & Colman
Royal Bank of Scotland	Unilever	United News &
United Utilities	Woolwich	Media

4.1.1 Sample and methodology

This survey, like previous surveys in this series, is an informal survey. It does not purport to apply any rigorous academic methodology in either selection or analysis; it does however give a broadbrush picture of current reporting trends, and the sample selected covers most sectors and represents 20 per cent of all FTSE 100 companies. At least 57 FTSE 100 companies currently produce summary financial statements, our sample therefore represents at least 35 per cent of such companies.

The sample was self-selecting. Those companies that were known to issue summary financial statements on the basis of previous surveys were approached and the 20 selected were the first 20 to be received. The sample is therefore biased towards those that have issued summary financial statements in the past and against those that have issued summary financial statements for the first time in the current period.

4.1.2 Previous surveys

In reviewing these summary financial statements, the conclusions of previous surveys in respect of the amount of information included by companies were confirmed; all companies appeared to be publishing information considerably in excess of what is required by law. Furthermore, many companies are clearly using the summary financial statement as a corporate brochure, as well as a means of communication with shareholders. The summary financial statement itself takes up a few pages at the back of the document, the bulk being taken up with a narrative review of activities and performance, and other information about the company.

4.1.3 Period covered

The summary financial statements inspected were dated between 30 September 1998 and 31 March 1999. There were no changes in regulation pertaining to summary financial statements between 30 September 1998 and the date of publication.

4.2 Summary of survey results

	No.	%
Summary statements (see **4.3.1**)		
Profit and loss account and balance sheet only	7	35
Profit and loss account, balance sheet and cash flow statement	7	35
Statement of total recognised gains and losses	3	15
Other [1]	3	15
	20	**100**

[1] E.g., profit and loss account, balance sheet, cash flow statement and reconciliation of movement in shareholders' funds.

46

	No.	%
Other financial information (see **4.3.2**)		
Reconciliation of movement on shareholders' funds	7	35
Notes	3	15
'Segmental information' heading	2	10
EPS – basic	20	100
EPS – headline	10	50
EPS – fully diluted	9	45
Narrative (see **4.3.3**)		
Chairman's statement	20	100
Chief executive's statement	15	75
Operating review	18	90
Financial review	8	40
Directors' report	6	30
Directors' report with reference to other information	11	55
Directors and their remuneration (see **4.3.4**)		
Statutory minimum only (total with comparative)	3	15
Table of basic salary, fees and bonus for individual directors	17	85
Pension details for individual directors	7	35
Details of interests in shares/share options for individual directors	8	40
Detail of gains/potential gains on the exercise of share options	4	20
Directors' biographies	20	100
Other statements (see **4.3.5**)		
Statement on achievement of targets	5	25
Corporate governance statements	13	65
Corporate governance statements cross-referenced to other information	5	25
Statutory warnings	20	100
Statutory warnings – highly visible	7	35
Prominent reference to Y2K and/or the euro	9	45
Statement on the environment	9	45
Statement on community activities	10	50
Analysis of shareholders	6	30

	No.	%
Timeliness (see **4.3.6**)		
Summary financial statements issued within 60 days	12	60
Summary financial statements issued between 60 and 90 days	8	40
	20	100
Presentation (see **4.3.7**)		
A4 or similar format	15	75
Index	16	80
Extensive use of graphics/photographs/ promotional-style material	4	20
Description of report as 'review and summary financial statement'	10	50
Description or report as 'review'	8	40
Financial highlights – 2/3 year comparatives	6	30
Financial highlights – 4/5 year comparatives	9	45
Financial highlights – tabular information	11	55
Financial highlights – bar and/or pie charts	14	70
Financial highlights – narrative information only	3	15
Mission statement	7	35
Statement on use of recycled/environmentally friendly papers and inks	12	60
Reference to corporate website	16	80
Statement by auditors (see **4.3.8**)		
Covering substantially all information in the document	1	5
Covering summary financial statements, including directors' report	5	25
Covering details of directors' remuneration beyond statutory minimum	9	45
Length (see **4.3.9**)		
1–20 pages	5	25
20–30 pages	5	25
30–40 pages	7	35
40 pages +	3	15
	20	100

4.3   Observations

The first general observation relates to the length and glossy nature of all the summary financial statements inspected, in contrast to the shorter and more basic summary financial statements issued by the remaining building societies. Whilst there was little variation in the overall quality of presentation of these summary financial statements, there were wide variations in content. There appeared to be little correlation between the length of documents and the volume of financial information disclosed, and it was something of a surprise to note that some of the best of the non-statutory 'additional' disclosures were provided by companies issuing relatively short documents that included a substantial amount of promotional-type material.

4.3.1   Financial statements

Most companies provided more than the statutory minimum (a summary profit and loss account, balance sheet and directors' report). Despite the fact that companies are now permitted to use headings other than those prescribed by statute, no company did so, although three companies, BOC, NatWest and Rank, had made an attempt to explain the meaning of some or all of the headings in the margins next to the headings. NatWest, for example, explains 'minority interests' as 'the interests of other people who hold shares in our subsidiary companies'. A cursory review of the related annual report for a handful of companies revealed that most were extracting the figures and headings directly from the full financial statements and into the summary financial statement, with minimal, if any adjustments.

4.3.2   Other financial information

Only three companies provided 'notes' to the summary financial statement covering matters such as accounting policies, the calculation of earnings per share, restatements due to changes in accounting policies and segmental information. Many companies included some of this information as footnotes to the summary financial statement.

Segmental information was provided by two companies under the heading 'segmental information'. However, most other companies provided some segmental information within the chief executive's statement, operating or financial review. The operating review was often divided into geographical and/or business segments and many companies provided operating and financial data (such as turnover and operating profits) on that basis.

There were significant variations in the disclosure of earnings per share. All companies included the basic figure but more companies disclosed a 'headline' figure than a fully diluted figure. The 'headline' figure was commonly described as 'before exceptional items' and companies explained the need for this information as a means of smoothing out the effects of distortions. A few companies explained how the basic figure was calculated; very few attempted to explain the calculation of the fully diluted figure.

4.3.3   *Narrative*

There are no statutory or other requirements either for statements by chairmen or chief executives, or for operating or financial reviews. The legislation requires a review of the performance of the business and likely future developments, but this requirement can be satisfied without the lengthy statements and reviews that are universally included in practice.

All companies included a chairman's statement and photograph of the chairman; only three did not carry a facsimile signature. However, only four chairmen's statements were dated. Of the 15 chief executives' statements, 14 were accompanied by a photograph. The chief executive's statement was always consistent with the chairman's statement in respect of signatures and dating. The figures given include two companies that issued a joint chairman's and chief executive's statement (National Grid and Cadbury Schweppes).

Most companies included some sort of operating review, but only two companies referred to it as an operating review. 'Business review', 'regional review', and 'category review' are just a few of the terms that were used to describe this narrative which was often in fact, a mixed operating and financial review. Only eight companies included a separately identified financial review; however, as we have noted, some companies included financial information in the 'business' or 'regional' review, and others included it in the directors' report. The form and content of the full annual report is probably the main determinant in these matters.

Most companies included a short section entitled 'directors' report'. The three that did not use that title clearly included the information required by statute within the published document, in one case under the heading 'Introduction'. In the two other cases, the information could be found in different parts of the document.

To satisfy the requirement noted above for a review of performance and likely future developments, the majority of companies referred in the directors' report either to information elsewhere in the document containing the summary financial statement (either by name or page numbers), or to information in another document containing statutory information, that accompanied the summary financial statement.

There were variations in the extent to which auditors included information in the directors' report within the scope of their examination. For only six companies was the directors' report specifically included in the scope of the auditors' examination. For the remaining 12 companies that included a separately identifiable directors' report, the directors' report was specifically excluded from the auditors' examination. The companies that did not make cross-references to other information in the directors' report were not necessarily the companies whose auditors included the report in the scope of their examination.

4.3.4   Directors and their remuneration

This area displayed the greatest disparities in both reporting practice and in the extent to which auditors had included information within the scope of their review. Companies are generally selective about the information that is extracted from the full annual report in this area and disclosures in the summary financial statements ranged from a single total with comparative (the statutory minimum) to over two full pages of information covering policy and data on pensions, shares, share options, the gains thereon and performance-related issues. A minority of companies referred to the full annual report for further details.

All companies included the statutory minimum information; however, the auditors of some companies did not include any information relating to directors' remuneration within the scope of their examination. Where auditors did include such information within the scope of their review, it tended to cover totals, rather than detailed information relating to individual directors. Of the 17 companies that gave a table of basic salary, fees and bonuses for individual directors, only four were included within the scope of the auditors' examination.

Only three companies disclosed the statutory minimum and no additional information. Several companies included detailed information on salaries, fees and bonuses but only gave totals for pension contributions. Most companies that gave details on directors' interests in shares also gave information on directors' share options and a few gave information on actual or potential gains on the exercise of those options. The auditors of only one company included detailed information on shares, share options or the gains thereon within the scope of their examination.

All companies included biographies of directors and 15 of the 20 companies included photographs of directors.

4.3.5   Other statements

A few companies that had publicly set themselves targets, in terms of returns to investors or growth in the value of their investments, reported on progress towards those targets.

Corporate governance statements ranged from a few paragraphs with references to the Cadbury, Hampel and other reports, to detailed explanations of corporate governance policies. There were several references to the full annual report for further details.

The statutory warning to the effect that the full annual accounts and directors' report should be consulted for a full understanding of the financial position appeared in many different places. A total of seven such statements were placed at the front of the document, four of them highly visible (i.e., in bold or large type, or inside a box). A total of nine such statements were placed at the front of the summary financial statements (which normally appeared at the back of the document), two of them highly visible, and a total of four such statements appeared at the back of the document, one being highly visible. In two cases, the statement was made twice, once at the front of the document and again before the summary financial statement.

Reference to the availability of the full annual accounts and directors' report was often made in the director's report. Nine companies made reference to the Y2K issue, four made reference to the euro, and several made full-page references to actions taken, or to be taken, on environmental issues and action in the community.

4.3.6 Timeliness

The majority of companies issued their summary financial statement within 60 days of the period-end. The average number of days between the period-end and the date of the summary financial statement was 57.

4.3.7 Presentation

Companies that used a non-A4 format tended to use a smaller, rather than a larger format, with the exception of Rank, which issued a folded sheet of A3. Woolwich used an A4 landscape format. All summary financial statements were glossy and made use of graphics and photographs. A high number of companies appeared to include photographs of their own staff, and in some cases stated the name of the person and the position they held within the company. Some companies made considerably more use of graphics, photographs and promotional-style material than others. Such companies included more material about their activities, products and services than others, which appeared to be directed as much towards potential customers as towards private investors. Such companies detailed the additional benefits of owning shares (such as discounts on products and services) and included relatively little 'hard' information on activities and performance in the current period. In the author's opinion, four companies fell into this category, two particularly good examples being British Telecom and Woolwich.

Summary financial statements are often directed at a wide audience; they are sometimes sent to all company employees, and to outsiders in response to general enquiries for information about the company. The information needs of those parties are met (at least in part) by the summary financial statement.

The layout of the document generally followed a variation on the following theme:

(a)   financial highlights;

(b)   chairman's statement;

(c)   chief executive's statement;

(d)   operational/business/ regional/category review;

(e)   financial review;

(f)   directors' report;

(g)   auditors' report;

(h)   summary financial statement; and

(i)   shareholder information.

There were considerable variations from this pattern; for example, the British Telecom document had the summary financial statement towards the front of the document and the auditors' report at the back.

Most companies included some financial highlights, normally on the inside cover or the first page. Some companies included them on the front cover or two or three pages into the document. The use of tables, bar charts and pie charts was not restricted to financial highlights, they sometimes also appeared in the operating or financial review to show growth in markets, market share, or profitability.

4.3.8 Statement by auditors

The auditors' statement tended to appear in one of two places: either immediately before the summary financial statement, or immediately after it. Twelve companies included the auditors' statement before, eight included it after the summary financial statement. Some auditors' reports referred to information dotted around the document, as included within the scope of the examination.

As noted in Chapter 3 above, auditors currently have a choice of statement formats. The auditor of only one company used the format suggested by SAS 600 *Auditors' Reports on Financial Statements*. The remainder used the format suggested by Practice Note 8 *Reports by Auditors Under Company Legislation in the United Kingdom*. Five statements were addressed to the shareholders, 15 were addressed to members.

4.3.9 Length

The longest report was that produced by Unilever, at 64 pages. The average number of pages in a report was 31. The shortest reports were produced by Lloyds TSB and Woolwich at 13 and 15 pages respectively. These companies have millions, rather than hundreds of thousands of shareholders and are more likely to make cost savings by issuing summary financial statements than companies with smaller share registers.

The number of pages occupied by the summary financial statement never exceeded 50 per cent of the total; in most cases, the summary financial statement took up about 20 per cent of the total.

CHAPTER 5

Comparison: seven summary financial statements

5.1 General

5.1.1 Selection criteria

The seven FTSE 100 companies selected for comparison were intended to represent a cross-section of industry and styles of reporting. The documents selected included relatively short formats with a substantial amount of general information, graphics and a limited amount of financial information, and longer documents with more financial information and narrative. The documents are intended to demonstrate the wide variety of reporting formats, all representing a high standard of reporting. Extracts are reproduced in Appendix 3.

5.1.2 Period covered

All seven summary financial statements covered the year to 31 December 1998 with the exception of Pilkington and BT, which covered the year to 31 March 1999, and Reckitt & Colman, which covered the 52 weeks to 2 January 1999.

5.2   Length

	Numbered pages
Rank	13
Pilkington	28
NatWest	28
British Telecom	49
Reckitt & Colman	36
Orange	32
Unilever	64

5.3   *Financial and operating highlights*

The presentation of financial highlights, together with comparatives, are clearly influenced by results. Highlights are often the first
item that readers are likely to encounter when reading the summary
financial statement and their presentation is therefore important.
Some companies' financial highlights appear a few pages into the
document, several include five-year summaries at the end.

	Narrative	*Graphics*
Rank	• No financial highlights given at the front of the document • Operational highlights given in acting chief executive's review • Five-year record of turnover, operating profit, earnings per share and dividends per share given in the finance director's review	• None

	Narrative	Graphics
Pilkington	• Brief narrative detailing operational highlights	• Table of turnover, operating profit, pre-tax profit and earnings per share, with percentage movements
NatWest	• Brief narrative elaborating on the bar chart	• Bar chart (overlaid on photographs of staff and customers) detailing five-year profit before tax, earnings per share, return on share-holders' funds and dividends per share
British Telecom	• None	• None
Reckitt & Colman	• Turnover, profit before tax, proposed dividend, dividend growth, action plan to address performance issues	• None
Orange	• None	• Table of turnover, operating profit/loss before tax, net cash inflow, loss per share with comparatives
Unilever	• Commentary on bar charts	• Bar charts detailing five-year turnover, operating profit, earnings and dividends per share; turnover and operating profit by region

5.4 Presentation

Current trends in presentation mean that directors tend to be photographed individually, rather than in a group, and in black and white, rather than in colour. Designers mix black-and-white and coloured graphics, and photographs of reasonably photogenic staff and customers are included as well as models. Despite this, each group seeks to convey its own corporate image and is constrained by the need to get a particular message across; variations in presentation year on year are common as groups develop their reporting styles.

5.4.1 Rank

This summary financial statement was the only one of the 20 surveyed in Chapter 4 to be presented in a folded A3 format, although other groups, including Whitbread use this format. Full use was made of colour, together with what appear to be a mixture of library photographs and photographs of customers and staff. Rather than mixing photographs and narrative, with the exception of the first few pages of narrative devoted to the chairman's and acting chief executive's review, each full page of photographs faced a full page of narrative. Photographs of the chairman, acting chief executive, the finance director and members of the board were individual photographs, in black and white, providing contrast and balance to the other 'fun' photographs and facts about the number of ice creams, holidays and pints of beer sold during the year. The back page was devoted to group brands and a substantial amount of information was given elsewhere relating to business structure and segmental information. As with all of the summary financial statements reviewed in the previous chapter, the statutory headings were used for the financial statements, but a useful glossary was provided in the margins to the financial statements, explaining some of the less well understood financial terms such as exceptional items and earnings per share.

The order of presentation was slightly unusual in that the financial statements were presented towards the front of the document under the heading 'How the figures look' followed by the finance director's review. The statutory warning relating to the sufficiency of the information in the summary financial statements and the availability of the full financial statements was also given in the directors' report.

5.4.2 *Pilkington*

This compact document printed on medium-weight paper made limited but stylish use of black and white photographs against a green and white colour scheme. The photograph of directors was a group photograph. Narrative on the front cover referred to targets and performance against those targets and the emphasis through-out the document was on the improvement of competitiveness and performance. Most pages contained narrative at the top and photo-graphs or graphics at the bottom, maintaining interest without distracting the reader from the substance of the text. The statutory warning was given at the back of the document in bold type.

5.4.3 *NatWest*

This document was typical of many in the financial sector with the use of glossy photographs and details of (real) staff and customers towards the beginning of the document, followed by a moderately detailed summary financial statement. The subtle separation of the two parts of the document by the use of a slightly different layout or font that is present in many documents was not present in this document which moved seamlessly from one part to the other. Photographs of directors were individual photographs and in colour, perhaps emphasising the human face of the bank. The emphasis throughout the document was on the services provided to customers and, in particular, business customers. The document would again be of interest to employees and the general public as well as investors. The statutory warning was included under the heading 'Important notice to shareholders' at the beginning of the document.

The narrative sections of the document were awarded the Crystal Mark by the Plain English Campaign.

5.4.4   British Telecom

This relatively thick little booklet was clearly directed towards a broad range of private shareholders, and others. On the face of it, there appeared to be very little financial information and a lot of photographs that caught the eye. On closer inspection however, the balance between narrative and graphics seemed more even; two pages of narrative were followed by a double page photograph. The level of detail given in the narrative belied the somewhat lightweight impression given by the document overall. The summary financial statement appeared immediately after the chairman's statement, much further forward in the document than in most (as with Rank). The research referred to in Chapter 2 showed that there is a direct relationship between the likelihood of something being read and its proximity to the front of the document; as such, this should encourage readers who might not otherwise do so, to read the financial statements. The financial statements as presented (profit and loss account and balance sheet) were straightforward and short, but the statutory terminology was used, and even the relatively sophisticated might struggle with 'group's share of ventures' turnover' and 'minority interests'. The remainder of the statutory information appeared at the back of the document. The emphasis throughout the document was on improvements to the quality of life facilitated by communications technology. BT is not 'just a telephone company'. Extracts from the summary financial statement were available on audio cassette for the benefit of the blind and partially sighted.

5.4.5   Reckitt & Colman

This document was representative of the medium to long category, with substantial narrative and financial information. Printed on heavyweight paper with mixed black and white, colour, small, and large photographs, the document attempted to convey a cohesive visual corporate message with the company's various products and markets. The information presented appeared to be balanced and comprehensive, and included a double 'regional' and 'category' review, covering both operational and financial matters. An attractive double cover opened out to give product information. The summary financial statement was clearly separated from the 'review' section of the document by the use of a cover page headed 'Accounts'; the statutory warning appeared before the directors' report headed 'Important note'.

5.4.6 *Orange*

Orange was selected on the basis that it is a relatively new company (to the UK), with little experience in the production of summary financial statements. This document, in black, white and orange was visually impressive. Each page of narrative faced a full page photograph selected for its relevance to corporate objectives rather than any direct relevance to products and services (e.g., grinning small boy holding a crab equals 'success'). There was an emphasis on youth, growth, progress and the future, and an attempt was made to explain the rapidly changing world of mobile telephone markets to the reader by means of a fold-out analysis of the European market at the front of the document, and a glossary of terms at the back. The document contained a substantial section on directors' remuneration and there was no clear distinction between the review and the summary financial statement. The statutory warning appeared in the directors' report.

5.4.7 *Unilever*

This was the longest document selected and is representative not only of its sector but of those groups that are required to report under other jurisdictions (in this case the USA and Holland) as well as in the UK. Like Reckitt & Colman, the group analyses its performance by both region and category. Full use was made in this document of colour photographs of products, smiling people, and bar charts to illustrate the narrative throughout. The style was bright, cheerful, and family-oriented; some of the stylish documents produced by UK companies would probably not be acceptable in the US market.

5.5 Contents – in order of presentation

Rank	• *Chairman's statement:* 1 page general commentary[1] with photograph and highlighted quotes
	• *Chief executive's review:* 1 page financial commentary[2] with photograph
	• *Summary financial statement:* 1 page with auditors' statement and glossary of terms in the margins
	• *Finance director's review:* 1 page with photograph and segmental information
	• *Investment:* 1 page on investment in business segments
	• *Employees and customers:* 1 page, by business segment
	• *Brands:* 1 page
	• *Looking to the future:* 0.5 page
	• *Business structure:* 0.5 page with average number of employees, turnover and operating profit by segment
	• *Summary directors' report:* 0.5 page referring to other parts of the document
	• *Shareholder information, extracts from the remuneration report:* 1 page
	• *The board:* 1 page of biographies and photographs
Pilkington	• *Chairman's statement:* 2.5 page financial commentary with photograph, facsimile signature and highlighted quotes
	• *Chief executive's review:* 2 page general commentary, with photograph and facsimile signature
	• *Building products, automotive products and technical products, by geographical segment:* 4.5 page commentary

[1] 'General commentary' indicates a mixed financial and operational commentary.

[2] 'Financial commentary' indicates a predominantly financial commentary.

- *Environment and community:* 1.5 page
- *'Building one Pilkington':* 2 pages on culture change and communication
- *Pilkington 1999:* 2 pages on business activities
- *The board:* 2 pages of biographies and photographs
- *Summary directors' report:* 0.5 page referring to other parts of the document for the business review, and to the full annual report for corporate governance issues
- *Auditors' statement:* 0.5 page
- *Summary financial statement:* 6 pages with notes

NatWest
- *Chairman's statement:* 2 page general commentary with photograph and facsimile signature
- *Chief executive's review:* 13 page financial commentary (but including 9 pages of photographs detailing basic facts about the group) with photograph, facsimile signature and date
- *Group overview:* detailed profit and loss segmental information for companies and groups within the group
- *The board:* 2 pages of biographies and photographs
- *Directors' pay and benefits:* 1 page
- *Summary directors' report:* 0.5 page referring to other parts of the document
- *Auditors' statement:* 0.5 page
- *Summary financial statement and notes:* 4 pages with auditors' statement and glossary of terms in the margins
- *Information for shareholders:* 2 pages including analysis of shareholders and reference to the *Social impact review*

British Telecom
- *Chairman's message:* 2 page general commentary on the group's mission, key achievements and financial performance with photograph and facsimile signature
- *Summary financial statement:* 2 pages

- *Chief executive's statement:* 2 page general commentary with photograph and facsimile signature
- *'Net gain', 'The datawave', 'Your move', 'Home work', 'Wake-up call', 'See hear', 'Teach yourself', 'Community conscious':* commentaries on internet developments, communications technology, mobile communications, working from home, global communications networks, videoconferencing, education and community issues
- *The board:* 2 pages of biographies and photographs
- *Financial results:* 2 pages outlining business and geographical performance
- *Auditors' statement and other statutory information:* 0.5 page
- *Shareholder information:* 1 page

Reckitt & Colman

- *Chairman's statement:* 2 page general commentary with photograph and facsimile signature
- *Operating review:* 19 pages on a regional and category basis
- *Community involvement and environment review:* 2 pages
- *The board:* 2 pages of biographies and photographs
- *Financial review:* 3 pages with photograph and facsimile signature
- *Summary directors' report:* 0.5 page referring to other parts of the document and the full annual report in respect of corporate governance issues
- *Summary financial statement:* 4 pages with segmental analyses, and a detailed five-year summary
- *Auditors' statement:* 0.5 page
- *Information for shareholders:* 0.5 page

Orange

- *Chairman's report:* 1 page general commentary with photograph

- *Chief executive's review:* 1 page general commentary with photograph
- *Business review:* 5 pages of operational information
- *Finance director's report:* 1 page with bar charts
- *Summary directors' report:* 1 page referring to corporate governance issues and other parts of the document in respect of the business review
- *Summary remuneration report:* 2 page detailed report on policy as well as remuneration with reference to the full annual report
- *The board:* 2 pages of biographies and photographs
- *Summary financial statement:* 2 pages
- *Auditors' statement:* 1 page
- *Analysis of shareholders and financial calendar:* 1 page
- *Shareholder information:* 1 page
- *5-year summary:* 1 page profit and loss account and balance sheet
- Glossary of terms: 1 page

Unilever
- *Joint chairmen's statement:* 6 page general commentary (categories, regions and prospects) with photographs and facsimile signatures
- *Financial highlights:* (see **5.3** above)
- *Business overview:* 23 pages on a regional basis and dealing with technology, Y2K, responsible corporate behaviour, and environmental responsibilities
- *Categories:* 12 pages
- *Financial review:* 5 pages
- *Organisation:* 1 page
- *The board:* 3 pages of biographies and photographs
- *Corporate governance statement:* 3 pages
- *Summary financial statements:* 4 pages including an introductory section referring to other parts of the document and including the auditors' statement
- *Financial calendar and shareholder information:* 2 pages

All groups included a financial calendar and website address. Nat-West, British Telecom and Reckitt & Colman's summary financial statements were printed on environmentally friendly paper. Full information on how to contact the various operating entities, with numerous addresses, telephone and fax numbers and websites were provided by Rank, Orange and Unilever.

5.6 Financial statements – in order of presentation

Rank	• 2 profit and loss accounts (including earnings per share) showing results before and after exceptional items • Balance sheet • Cash flow statement • Signed by chairman and finance director, 48 days after period-end • Summary directors' report
Pilkington	• Profit and loss account (including earnings per share and fully diluted earnings per share) • Balance sheet • Cash flow statement • Statement of total recognised gains and losses • Reconciliation of movement in shareholders' funds • Summary group cash flow statement • Notes: accounting policies, segmental information/results of continuing operations, net assets of continuing operations, exceptional items, net borrowings, directors' remuneration
NatWest	• Profit and loss account (including earnings per share, fully diluted and headline earnings per share) • Statement of total recognised gains and losses • Balance sheet • Cash flow statement

- Reconciliation of movement in shareholders funds
- Notes: accounting policies, provision for bad debts, profit on sale of business, profit by segment, tax, dividends, earnings per share, litigation
- Signed by chairman, chief executive and chief financial officer, 53 days after period-end

British Telecom
- Profit and loss account (including earnings per share and headline earnings per share)
- Balance sheet
- Signed by chairman, chief executive and finance director, 56 days after period-end

Reckitt & Colman
- Profit and loss account (including fully diluted earnings per share)
- Balance sheet
- Cash flow statement
- Segmental analysis of results on a regional and category basis
- Five-year summary profit and loss account and balance sheet
- Signed by chairman, chief executive and finance director, 42 days after period-end

Orange
- Profit and loss account (including loss per share)
- Balance sheet
- Reconciliation of movement in shareholders' funds
- Cash flow statement

Unilever
- Profit and loss account (including earnings per share and fully diluted earnings per share)
- Balance sheet
- Cash flow statement
- Signed by joint chairmen, 67 days after period-end

5.7 *Auditors' examination*

As noted in Chapter 4, there are considerable variations in the scope of the auditors' examination.

	Scope of auditors' statement	*Position of statement*
Rank	• Financial statements only	• Before financial statements
Pilkington	• Financial statements and notes only	• Before financial statements
NatWest	• Financial statements and notes only	• Before financial statements
British Telecom	• Financial statements, directors' biographies and financial results	• End of report, after and separated from financial statements
Reckitt & Colman	• Financial statements and segmental analysis only	• After financial statements
Orange	• Financial statements only	• After financial statements
Unilever	• Financial statements and introductory narrative only	• Before financial statements

CHAPTER 6

Case histories: four companies

6.1   General

Four FTSE 100 companies were approached, and telephone interviews were conducted or a questionnaire was sent to company secretaries. A number of general questions were asked about the company's experience in the production of summary financial statements and a number of specific questions were asked about the most recent summary financial statement. The four companies were the Rank Group, Orange, Unilever and National Power. The general questions included the following:

(a)   what, if any, are the main weaknesses in the current regulatory framework (s251 CA 1985 and SI 1995 No 2092)? How could the regulatory framework be improved?

(b)   please describe the primary user group for summary financial statements. What advice has the group taken on the content and design of summary financial statements? Has the group undertaken any research into recipient satisfaction or understanding? Has the content or design of summary financial statements changed as a result of this?

6.1.1   Regulatory framework

The regulatory framework was not considered a significant issue for any of the companies surveyed; however, one company felt that the regime was too flexible in that it permitted the company's less scrupulous competitors to present less balanced information than might have been required by a tighter regime. Another company felt that the system for ascertaining the wishes of shareholders in respect of the receipt of summary financial statements was wasteful; most private shareholders were felt to be indifferent to the issue and full information would always be available to those shareholders who did wish to receive it.

6.1.2 Users

All companies placed considerable emphasis on informal feedback received from private shareholders at annual general meetings. Shareholders were typically retired, actively interested in the company and had a moderate or high level of financial awareness (although it was conceded that such shareholders are not necessarily representative of private shareholders). Only one company had conducted any formal research into the views of users but it had been unable to make any changes to the report for administrative reasons.

6.1.3 Auditors' statement

Three companies considered the auditors' statement to be valuable, one company thought that the majority of shareholders would not notice if the auditors' statement were to disappear. No company considered the processes applied by auditors to be of significant benefit, or additional cost to the company.

Company-specific information is set out below.

6.2 Rank Group plc

The Rank Group's assets include the Hard Rock brand, Odeon Cinemas, Butlins, Mecca Bingo, Pinewood Studios and Grosvenor Casinos. It first issued summary financial statements in 1993 and has done so continuously since then. For the first two years, two books were produced, but there was a substantial degree of duplication and the summary was felt to be too long. Over the years, the summary has become shorter, rather than longer. The current folded A3 format was introduced in 1997 and is felt to be a success; it contains less information overall than previous documents, but the company believes that the information is more likely to be read as a result. The inclusion in the summary financial statement of a small glossary of terms towards the front of the document (rather than at the back) is also intended to encourage readers who would otherwise rely on the financial highlights (absent from the current document) to try to understand the financial statements. The use of headings other than the statutory headings in the summary financial statement was considered to be potentially confusing. Despite the fact that the auditors' statement was delegated to the margin (as one of the least read sections of the summary financial statement in practice) the company considers the inclusion of the statement to be essential; without it, the document would lack credibility.

In previous summary financial statements the full remuneration report had been included; this year an extract had been provided. Shareholders at the AGM had indicated that many did not understand the complex pension arrangements described in the report. The information was available in the annual report for anyone who required it and the group took the decision to include extracts in the summary financial statement (very few companies reproduce the full remuneration report in the summary financial statements).

The business review in previous summary financial statements had dealt with each part of the group separately. The current format takes a more integrated view of the group and deals with each part under the themes of 'investment', 'employees and customers', 'brands' and ' . . . looking to the future'.

Rank has approximately 75,000 shareholders, although 97 per cent of the company's capital is held by institutions. All shareholders receive the summary financial statement and approximately 40,000 copies of the full annual report are printed. Net cost savings are achieved by the production of summary financial statements, despite the increase in administration costs arising from the production of two documents.

6.3   Orange plc

Orange plc provides mobile communications services in Europe. It is 49 per cent owned by Hutchinson Whampoa and has 1.2bn shares in issue. Its private shareholders represent 88 per cent in number of total shareholders and they hold 1.1 per cent by value of the company's shares. The company sends its new shareholders a 'welcome pack', informing them of the availability of the full annual report together with a pre-paid reply card. Approximately 1,000 requests for the full annual report have been received each year.

Orange first issued summary financial statements in 1997, the year after it was floated in the UK; it was felt that this was appropriate for a communications company. The company has experienced an increase in the costs of reporting as a result of the decision to issue the summary financial statement and does not expect those costs to decrease significantly in the future. These costs arise mainly from the administrative time involved in setting up the templates, and considering the design of the report and the considerable effort of consulting on what should be included. Those involved in the production of the document meet with all members of executive management as well as groups of employees as part of this process. The summary financial statement is sent to all employees as well as private shareholders and sometimes doubles as a corporate brochure.

The company includes market information, a glossary of terms, information about the group structure, an analysis of shareholdings and fairly basic financial statements with no notes, with a view to informing and educating. The market information and glossary of terms in particular are included to provide some background and context for shareholders.

A relatively long remuneration report is included, similar to the report included in the full annual report. It is felt that shareholders would prefer this information to be included rather than excluded, despite its complexity, and inclusion has the added advantage of heading off questions at the AGM.

It is not thought that a significant number of private shareholders read the financial statements and what is included does not contain notes or a significant amount of explanatory material; it is considered that the financial highlights are more important to most private shareholders in this respect.

6.4 *Unilever*

Unilever comprises two legal entities, Unilever plc and Unilever NV, which operate as far as possible as a single business but which have separate sets of shareholders.

Unilever has considerable experience in the production of summary financial statements: they were first produced in 1991 when the legislation was introduced to permit them, although the company had been producing, and sending to all shareholders, a two-part annual report for some years before that. Unilever produces its annual review (and its full annual report) in English for its UK, US (and other) shareholders (sterling and guilder versions) and Dutch for its Dutch shareholders (guilder version only). Only one basic report is produced, translated and adjusted for currency impacts; the annual review therefore needs to comply with regulation and best practice in all three countries. Dutch shareholders in particular are not yet accustomed to the brief, PR-style documents that are produced by some UK companies and this accounts for the relatively lengthy nature of the document (64 pages). It also accounts for the absence of overt references to the Cadbury Committee in the context of corporate governance (not relevant outside the UK) and the relatively small amount of information on directors' remuneration (not yet required or considered appropriate in Holland). Full corporate governance information and information on directors' remuneration is given in the second, annual accounts volume.

Unilever plc has approximately 100,000 shareholders; less than two per cent are institutional shareholders, but they hold 85 per cent by value of the company's shares. All shareholders receive the annual review. Under seven per cent of shareholders are in receipt of the full annual report. Unilever plc set up its system for ascertaining shareholders' wishes under the old regulations which required that companies send both the full annual report and the summary financial statement to shareholders; it has so far proved easier to let that system continue. With multiple language and currency publications and a range of mailing destinations, the distribution of Unilever Report and Accounts is already a complex operation.

There were additional costs in setting up systems to produce and distribute summary financial statements. Since then, the production of summary financial statements has been broadly cost neutral to the company. The company views the object of sending the summary financial statements to be improved communication with private shareholders and accepts that only companies with a larger number of shareholders and producing much shorter summary financial statements are likely to make clear cost savings.

6.5   *National Power*

National Power has produced summary financial statements since it was privatised and floated in 1991. It has approximately 800,000 shareholders, all of whom receive the summary financial statement and approximately 50,000 of whom request the full report and accounts. A number of brokers and analysts, PEP companies, and the FT Annual Reports Club also request the full report and accounts. All employee shareholders receive the summary financial statement.

There are a number of shareholders who ask the company not to send them any financial information at all. While the company encourages shareholder interest in its business at all levels, it considers that the statutory framework might be improved by introducing the possibility of a formal 'opt-out' for such shareholders, which would enable a more efficient use of resources.

The summary financial statement and the report and accounts are written with different audiences in mind. The summary financial statement is designed to be a relatively low cost, straightforward document attractive to the lay reader rather than the financial community. Efforts are made to use plainer English in the summary financial statement and the company has regard to certain matters that other companies with a smaller number of private shareholders might not, for example, print size and the volume of information on a single page. The company receives feedback from shareholders regarding the nature and content of the summary financial statement, and takes on board practicable suggestions, where possible; however, given the very large shareholder base at present, it would not be an efficient use of resources to conduct separate research into shareholder views on the summary financial statement.

It is company policy to submit the production of the report (and many other services) to competitive tender. Tight cost control policies require that the cost of the production of the summary financial statement is contained at least within inflationary levels. The environmentally friendly paper, inks and packaging used for production are ordered well in advance in order to achieve this.

The summary financial statement is produced to a tight timetable. The summary financial statement and report and accounts are produced a month after the preliminary announcement of annual results and the company's AGM is held one month after that. The company is aware that a number of companies aim to report more quickly than this and supports this in principle. However, the volume of production involved currently mitigates against this. While the preliminary announcement of results is not routinely mailed to shareholders, it is available on request and via the company's web site. It also forms the basis of the business review of the summary financial statement.

Considerable space is devoted to directors' remuneration. Of a total 24 pages in the current summary financial statement, eight pages are devoted to the company's business review of the year and four pages relate to directors' remuneration. This is a reduction compared with earlier years (partly at the request of shareholders) but still achieves full compliance with relevant governance codes.

Photographs of directors are generally not provided. They are very costly to produce each year and disproportionately so within the overall budget. No cash flow statement is currently produced, most shareholders wishing to concentrate attention on the familiar profit and loss account. Two pages are devoted to corporate governance and employee matters which is considered necessary and appropriate for a company such as National Power.

Legal requirements

Section 251 Companies Act 1985

Listed public companies

251.—(1) A public company whose share or debentures, or any class of whose shares or debentures, are listed need not, in such cases as may be specified by regulations made by the Secretary of State, and provided any conditions so specified are complied with, send copies of the documents referred to in section 238(1) to entitled persons, but may instead send them a summary financial statement.

In this section–

> "entitled persons", in relation to a company, means such of the persons specified in paragraphs (a) to (c) of subsection (1) of section 238 as are or would apart from this section be entitled to be sent copies of those documents relating to the company which are referred to in that subsection; and
> "listed" means admitted to the Official List of the International Stock Exchange of the United Kingdom and the Republic of Ireland Limited.

(2) Copies of the documents referred to in section 238(1) shall, however, be sent to any entitled person who wishes to receive them; and the Secretary of State may by regulations make provision as to the manner in which it is to be ascertained (whether before or after he becomes an entitled person) whether an entitled person wishes to receive them.

(3) The summary financial statement shall be derived from the company's annual accounts and the directors' report and shall be in such form and contain such information as may be specified by regulations made by the Secretary of State.

(4) Every summary financial statement shall—

> (a) state that it is only a summary of information in the company's annual accounts and the directors' report;

> (b) contain a statement by the company's auditors of their opinion as to whether the summary financial statement

is consistent with those accounts and that report and complies with the requirements of this section and regulations made under it;

(c) state whether the auditors' report on the annual accounts was unqualified or qualified, and if it was qualified set out the report in full together with any further material needed to understand the qualification;

(d) state whether the auditors' report on the annual accounts contained a statement under—

(i) section 237(2) (accounting records or returns inadequate or accounts not agreeing with records and returns), or

(ii) section 237(3) (failure to obtain necessary information and explanations),

and if so, set out the statement in full.

(5) Regulations under this section shall be made by statutory instrument which shall be subject to annulment in pursuance of a resolution of either House of Parliament.

(6) If default is made in complying with this section or regulations made under it, the company and every officer of it who is in default is guilty of an offence and liable to a fine.

(7) Section 240 (requirements in connection with publication of accounts) does not apply in relation to the provision to entitled persons of a summary financial statement in accordance with this section.

1995 No 2092

COMPANIES

The Companies (Summary Financial Statement) Regulations 1995

Made	*4th August 1995*
Laid before Parliament	*8th August 1995*
Coming into force	*1st September 1995*

ARRANGEMENT OF REGULATIONS

PART I

GENERAL

PART II

CONDITIONS FOR SENDING OUT SUMMARY FINANCIAL STATEMENT

PART III

FORM AND CONTENT OF SUMMARY FINANCIAL STATEMENT

PART IV

TRANSITIONALS ETC

11. Revocation, transitionals and saving.
12. Consequential amendments

SCHEDULES

Schedule 1 – Form and content of summary financial statement of companies and groups other than banking or insurance companies and groups

Schedule 2 – Form and content of summary financial statement of banking companies and groups

Schedule 3 – Form and content of summary financial statement of insurance companies and groups

The Secretary of State, in exercise of the powers conferred on him by sections 245(3) and (4) and 251(1), (2) and (3) of the Companies Act 1985 and of all other powers enabling him in that behalf, hereby makes the following Regulations:

PART I

GENERAL

Citation and commencement

1. These Regulations may be cited as the Companies (Summary Financial Statement) Regulations 1995 and shall come into force on 1st September 1995.

Interpretation

2. In these Regulations, unless otherwise stated–

"the 1985 Act" means the Companies Act 1985;

"banking company" means a company the directors of which prepare accounts for a financial year in accordance with the special provisions of Part VII of the 1985 Act relating to banking companies;

"EEA State" means a State which is a Contracting Party to the Agreement on the European Economic Area signed at Oporto on 2nd May 1992, as adjusted by the Protocol signed at Brussels on 17th March 1993 and by EEA Council Decision Number 1/95 of 10th March 1995;

"entitled persons" means the same as in section 251 of the 1985 Act;

"full accounts and reports" means a company's annual accounts, the directors' report and the auditors' report on those accounts required to be sent to entitled persons under section 238(1) of the 1985 Act and "full" in relation to any balance sheet, profit and loss account, group accounts or directors' report means any such document comprised in the full accounts and reports;

"insurance company" means a company the directors of which prepare accounts for a financial year in accordance with the special provisions of Part VII of the 1985 Act relating to insurance companies;

"listed public company" means a public company whose shares or debentures, or any class of whose shares or debentures, are listed within the meaning of section 251(1) of the 1985 Act.

PART II

CONDITIONS FOR SENDING OUT SUMMARY FINANCIAL STATEMENT

Cases in which sending of summary financial statement prohibited

3.—(1) A listed public company may not send a summary financial statement to an entitled person instead of copies of its full accounts and reports, in any case where it is prohibited from doing so by any relevant provision (within the meaning of paragraph (2) below)–

(a) in its memorandum or articles of association, or

(b) where the entitled person is a holder of the company's debentures, in any instrument constituting or otherwise governing any of the company's debentures of which that person is the holder.

(2) For the purposes of paragraph (1) above, any provision (however expressed) which requires copies of the full accounts and reports to be sent to entitled persons, or which forbids the sending of summary financial statements under section 251 of the 1985 Act, is a relevant provision.

Ascertainment of entitled person's wishes

4.—(1) A listed public company may not send a summary financial statement to an entitled person in place of copies of its full accounts and reports, unless the company has ascertained that the entitled person does not wish to receive copies of those documents.

(2) Whether or not an entitled person wishes to receive copies of the full accounts and reports for a financial year is to be ascertained–

(a) from any relevant notification in writing he has given to the company (either as an entitled person or as a person to whom paragraph (5) of this regulation applies) as to whether he wishes to receive copies of the full accounts and reports or as to whether he wishes, instead of copies of those documents, to receive summary financial statements; or

(b) failing any such express notification, from any failure to respond to an opportunity given to the entitled person (including for this purpose a person to whom paragraph (5) of this regulation applies) to elect to receive copies of the full accounts and reports either in response to a notice sent by the company under regulation (5) below, or as part of a relevant consultation of his wishes by the company under regulation (6) below.

(3) For the purposes of paragraph (2)(a) above, a notification is a relevant notification with respect to a financial year if it relates to that year (whether or not it has been given at the invitation of the company) and if it is received by the company not later than 28 days before the first date on which copies of the full accounts and reports are sent out to entitled persons in compliance with section 238(1) of the 1985 Act with respect to the financial year.

(4) A company may not send a summary financial statement to an entitled person in relation to any financial year in place of copies of the full accounts and reports unless–

(a) the period allowed for laying and delivering full accounts and reports under section 244 of the 1985 Act for that year has not expired;

(b) the summary financial statement has been approved by the board of directors and the original statement signed on behalf of the board by a director of the company.

(5) This paragraph applies to a person who is entitled, whether conditionally or unconditionally, to become an entitled person in relation to the company, but who has not yet become such an entitled person.

Consultation by notice

5.—(1) A listed public company may give notice to an entitled person (including for this purpose a person to whom regulation 4(5) above applies), by sending it by post or giving it in any other manner authorised by the company's articles, which shall–

(a) state that for the future, so long as he is an entitled person, he will be sent a summary financial statement for each financial year instead of a copy of the company's full accounts and reports, unless he notifies the company in writing that he wishes to receive full accounts and reports,

(b) state that the summary financial statement for a financial year will contain a summary of the company's or group's profit and loss account, balance sheet and directors' report for that year,

(c) state that the printed card or form accompanying the notice in accordance with paragraph (2) below must be returned by a date specified in the notice, being a date at least 21 days after service of the notice and not less than 28 days before the first date on which copies of the full accounts and reports for the next financial year for which the entitled person is entitled to receive them are sent out to entitled persons in compliance with section 238(1) of the 1985 Act,

(d) include a statement in a prominent position to the effect that a summary financial statement will not contain sufficient information to allow as full an understanding of the results and state of affairs of the company or group as would be provided by the full annual accounts and reports and that members and debenture holders requiring more detailed information have the right to obtain, free of charge, a copy of the company's last full accounts and reports, and

(e) state that the summary financial statement will contain a statement by the company's auditors as to whether the summary financial statement is consistent with the full accounts and reports for the year in question, whether it complies with the requirements of section 251 of the Act and of these Regulations and whether their report on the accounts was qualified.

(2) Subject to paragraph (3) below, the notice shall be accompanied by a printed card or form, in respect of which any postage necessary for its return to the company has been, or will be, paid by the company, which is so worded as to enable an entitled person (including a person to whom regulation 4(5) above applies), by marking a box and returning the card or form, to notify the company that he wishes to receive full accounts and reports for the next financial year for which he is entitled to receive them as an entitled person and for all future financial years thereafter.

(3) The company need not pay the postage in respect of the return of the printed card or form in the following circumstances–

   (a) if the address of a member to which notices are sent in accordance with the company's articles is not within an EEA State,

   (b) if the address of a debenture holder to which notices are sent in accordance with the terms of any instrument constituting or otherwise governing the debentures of which he is a holder is not within an EEA State, or

   (c) if the address of a person to whom regulation 4(5) above applies to which notices are sent, in accordance with the contractual provisions whereunder he has a right (conditionally or unconditionally) to become an entitled person, is not within an EEA State.

Relevant consultation

6.—(1) A listed public company may conduct a relevant consultation to ascertain the wishes of an entitled person.

(2) For the purposes of this regulation, a relevant consultation of the wishes of an entitled person is a notice given to the entitled person (including for this purpose a person to whom regulation 4(5) above applies), by sending it by post or giving it in any other manner authorised by the company's articles, which–

   (a) states that for the future, so long as he is an entitled person, he will be sent a summary financial statement instead of the full accounts and reports of the company, unless he notifies the company in writing that he wishes to continue to receive full accounts and reports;

   (b) accompanies a copy of the full accounts and reports;

   (c) accompanies a copy of the summary financial statement, prepared in accordance with section 251 of the 1985 Act and these Regulations, with respect to the financial year covered by those full accounts and reports and which is identified in the notice as an example of the document which the entitled person will receive for the future, so long as he is an entitled person, unless he notifies the company to the contrary; and

(d) subject to paragraph (3) below, is accompanied by a printed card or form, in respect of which any postage necessary for its return to the company has been, or will be, paid by the company, which is so worded as to enable an entitled person (including a person to whom regulation 4(5) above applies), by marking a box and returning the card or form, to notify the company that he wishes to receive full accounts and reports for the next financial year for which he is entitled to receive them as an entitled person and for all future financial years thereafter.

(3) Regulation 5(3) applies in respect of the payment of postage for the return of the printed card or form referred to in paragraph (2)(d) of this regulation.

PART III

FORM AND CONTENT OF SUMMARY FINANCIAL STATEMENT

Provisions applying to all companies and groups

7.—(1) Every summary financial statement issued by a listed public company in place of the full accounts and reports must comply with this regulation.

(2) The summary financial statement must state the name of the person who signed it on behalf of the board.

(3) The summary financial statement of a company which is not required to prepare group accounts under Part VII of the 1985 Act must include a statement in a prominent position to the effect that the summary financial statement does not contain sufficient information to allow for a full understanding of the results and state of affairs of the company as would be provided by the full annual accounts and reports, and that members and debenture

holders requiring more detailed information have the right to obtain, free of charge, a copy of the company's last full accounts and reports.

(4) The summary financial statement of a company which is required to prepare group accounts under Part VII of the 1985 Act must include a statement in a prominent position to the effect that the summary financial statement does not contain sufficient information to allow for a full understanding of the results of the group and state of affairs of the company or of the group as would be provided by the full annual accounts and reports, and that members and debenture holders requiring more detailed information have the right to obtain, free of charge, a copy of the company's last full accounts and reports.

(5) The summary financial statement must contain a clear, conspicuous statement–

(a) of how members and debenture holders can obtain, free of charge, a copy of the company's last full accounts and reports, and

(b) of how members and debenture holders may elect in writing to receive full accounts and reports in place of summary financial statements for all future financial years.

Companies and groups other than banking and insurance companies and groups

8.—(1) The summary financial statement of a listed public company (other than a banking or insurance company) the directors of which are not required to prepare group accounts under Part VII of the 1985 Act, shall be in the form, and contain the information, required by Schedule 1 to these Regulations so far as applicable to such a company.

(2) The summary financial statement of a listed public company (other than the parent company of a banking or insurance group) the directors of which are required to prepare group accounts under Part VII of the 1985 Act, shall be in the form, and contain the

information, required by Schedule 1 to these Regulations, so far as applicable to such a company.

Banking companies and groups

9.—(1) The summary financial statement of a listed public company which is in relation to the financial year in question a banking company the directors of which are not required to prepare group accounts under Part VII of the 1985 Act, shall be in the form, and contain the information, required by Schedule 2 to these Regulations, so far as applicable to such a company.

(2) The summary financial statement of a listed public company which is the parent company of a banking group shall be in the form, and contain the information, required by Schedule 2 to these Regulations, so far as applicable to such a company.

Insurance companies and groups

10.—(1) The summary financial statement of a listed public company which is in relation to the financial year in question an insurance company the directors of which are not required to prepare group accounts under Part VII of the 1985 Act, shall be in the form, and contain the information, required by Schedule 3 to these Regulations, so far as applicable to such a company.

(2) The summary financial statement of a listed public company which is the parent company of an insurance group shall be in the form, and contain the information, required by Schedule 3 to these Regulations, so far as applicable to such a company.

Revocation, transitionals and saving

11.—(1) The Companies (Summary Financial Statement) Regulations 1992 are hereby revoked.

(2) A listed public company other than one to which regulation 10 above applies may, with respect to a financial year of the company commencing on a date prior to 23rd December 1994, comply with the Companies (Summary Financial Statement) Regulations 1992 as though those Regulations had not been revoked by

paragraph (1) above, and accordingly need not comply with the provisions of these Regulations.

(3) Paragraph (4) below has effect in relation to the ascertainment of the wishes of an entitled person for the purposes of section 251(2) of the 1985 Act.

(4) So far as anything done under or for the purposes of any provision of the Companies (Summary Financial Statement) Regulations 1992 could have been done under or for the purposes of the corresponding provision of these Regulations, it is not invalidated by the revocation of that provision but has effect as if done under or for the purposes of the corresponding provision.

Consequential amendments

12.—(1) The Companies (Revision of Defective Accounts and Report) Regulations 1990 are amended as follows.

(2) *Words substituted in regulations 14(2) and (4) and 16(3)*

(3) After regulation 16(3) insert the following paragraph–

Paragraph inserted in regulation 16(3)

Phillip Oppenheim
Minister for Company Affairs,
Department of Trade and Industry.

4th August 1995

SCHEDULE 1

FORM AND CONTENT OF SUMMARY FINANCIAL STATEMENT OF COMPANIES AND GROUPS OTHER THAN BANKING OR INSURANCE COMPANIES AND GROUPS

Form of summary financial statement

1.—(1) The summary financial statement shall contain the information prescribed by the following paragraphs of this Schedule, in such order and under such headings as the directors consider appropriate, together with any other information necessary to ensure that the summary financial statement is consistent with the full accounts and reports for the financial year in question.

(2) Nothing in this Schedule shall be construed as prohibiting the inclusion in the summary financial statement of any additional information derived from the company's annual accounts and the directors' report.

Summary directors' report

2.—(1) The summary financial statement shall contain the whole of, or a summary of, that portion of the directors' report for the year in question which sets out the following matters–

(a) the matters required by section 234(1)(a) of the 1985 Act (business review);

(b) the amount recommended to be paid as dividend, if not disclosed in the summary profit and loss account;

(c) the matters required by paragraph 6(a) of Schedule 7 to the 1985 Act (important post-balance sheet events);

(d) the matters required by paragraph 6(b) of that Schedule (likely future developments in the business).

(2) The summary financial statement shall also contain the list of names of directors required by section 234(2) of the 1985 Act.

Summary profit and loss account: companies not required to prepare group accounts

3.—(1) The summary financial statement shall contain, in the case of a company the directors of which are not required to prepare group accounts for the financial year, a summary profit and loss account showing, in so far as they may be derived from the full profit and loss account, the following items, or combination of items, listed in sub-paragraph (3) below, in the order set out in that sub-paragraph.

(2) The items or combinations of items listed in sub-paragraph (3) below may appear under such headings as the directors consider appropriate.

(3) The items, or combination of items, referred to in sub-paragraph (1) above are–

   (a) turnover:
      —format 1, item 1
      —format 2, item 1
      —format 3, item B1
      —format 4, item B1;

   (b) income from shares in group undertakings and participating interests:
      the combination of the following two items
      —format 1, items 7 and 8
      —format 2, items 9 and 10
      —format 3, items B3 and B4
      —format 4, items B5 and B6;

   (c) other interest receivable and similar income and interest payable and similar charges:
      the net figure resulting from the combination of the following two items
      —format 1, items 10 and 12
      —format 2, items 12 and 14
      —format 3, items B6 and A5
      —format 4, items B8 and A7;

   (d) the profit or loss on ordinary activities before taxation;

   (e) tax on profit or loss on ordinary activities:
      —format 1, item 13
      —format 2, item 15
      —format 3, item A6
      —format 4, item A8;

   (f) profit or loss on ordinary activities after tax:
      —format 1, item 14
      —format 2, item 16
      —format 3, item A7 or B7
      —format 4, item A9 or B9;

(g) extraordinary income and charges after tax:
the net figure resulting from the combination of the
following items–
—format 1, items 17 and 18
—format 2, items 19 and 20
—format 3, items A8, A9 and B8
—format 4, items A10, A11 and B10;

(h) profit or loss for the financial year:
—format 1, item 20
—format 2, item 22
—format 3, item A11 or B9
—format 4, item A13 or B11; and

(i) the aggregate amount of dividends paid and, if not disclosed in the summary directors' report, proposed.

(4) The summary profit and loss account shall also show, at the
end thereof and under such heading as the directors consider
appropriate, the figure required by paragraph 1(1) of Part I of
Schedule 6 to the 1985 Act (directors' emoluments).

Summary profit and loss account: companies required to prepare group accounts

4.—(1) The summary financial statement shall contain, in the
case of a company the directors of which are required to prepare
group accounts for the financial year, a summary consolidated
profit and loss account showing the items or combinations of items
required by paragraph 3 above, in the order required by that paragraph and under such headings as the directors consider appropriate, but with the modifications specified in sub-paragraph (2)
below:

(2) The modifications referred to in sub-paragraph (1) above are
as follows–

(a) in place of the information required by paragraph
3(3)(b), there shall be shown, under such heading as the
directors consider appropriate, the item "Income from
interests in associated undertakings" required to be

shown in the Schedule 4 formats by paragraph 21(3) of Schedule 4A to the 1985 Act;

(b) between the information required by paragraph 3(3)(f) and that required by paragraph 3(3)(g) there shall in addition be shown, under such heading as the directors consider appropriate, the item "Minority interests" required to be shown in the Schedule 4 formats by paragraph 17(3) of Schedule 4A to the 1985 Act; and

(c) the figure required by paragraph 3(3)(g) shall be shown after the deduction or the addition (as the case may be) of the item "Minority interests" required to be shown in the Schedule 4 formats by paragraph 17(4) of Schedule 4A to the 1985 Act.

Summary balance sheet: companies not required to prepare group accounts

5.—(1) The summary financial statement shall contain, in the case of a company the directors of which are not required to prepare group accounts for the financial year, a summary balance sheet.

(2) Subject to sub-paragraphs (3) and (4) below, the summary balance sheet shall show, in so far as it can be derived from the full balance sheet and under such heading as the directors consider appropriate, a single amount for each of the headings to which letters are assigned in the balance sheet format which has been used for the full balance sheet (where necessary by the combination of the items to which Roman and Arabic numbers are assigned under those headings) in the order set out in the full balance sheet.

(3) Where an alternative position is permitted for any item in the balance sheet used, the summary balance sheet shall use the position used by the full balance sheet.

(4) Where the full balance sheet used is format 2 in Schedule 4 to the 1985 Act, then in the case of heading C under "Liabilities", two figures must be shown, one figure for amounts falling due within one year and one for amounts falling due after one year.

Summary balance sheet: companies required to prepare group accounts

6. The summary financial statement shall contain, in the case of a company the directors of which are required to prepare group accounts for the financial year, a summary consolidated balance sheet which shall show the items required by paragraph 5 above, in the order required by that paragraph and under such headings as the directors consider appropriate; but with the addition of the item "Minority interests" required by paragraph 17(2) of Schedule 4A to the 1985 Act, to be inserted as required by that paragraph.

Corresponding amounts

7. In respect of every item shown in the summary profit and loss account or summary consolidated profit and loss account (as the case may be), or in the summary balance sheet or summary consolidated balance sheet (as the case may be) the corresponding amount shall be shown for the immediately preceding financial year; for this purpose "the corresponding amount" is the amount shown in the summary financial statement for that year or which would have been so shown had such a statement been prepared for that year, after any adjustments necessary to ensure that that amount is comparable with the item for the financial year in question.

SCHEDULE 2

FORM AND CONTENT OF SUMMARY FINANCIAL STATEMENT OF BANKING COMPANIES AND GROUPS

Form of summary financial statement

1.—(1) The summary financial statement shall contain the information prescribed by the following paragraphs of this Schedule, in such order and under such headings as the directors consider appropriate, together with any other information necessary to ensure that the summary financial statement is consistent with the full accounts and reports for the financial year in question.

(2) Nothing in this Schedule shall be construed as prohibiting the inclusion in the summary financial statement of any additional

information derived from the company's annual accounts and the directors' report.

Summary directors' report

2.—(1) The summary financial statement shall contain the whole of, or a summary of, that portion of the directors' report for the year in question which sets out the following matters–

    (a) the matters required by section 234(1)(a) of the 1985 Act (business review);

    (b) the amount recommended to be paid as dividend, if not disclosed in the summary profit and loss account;

    (c) the matters required by paragraph 6(a) of Schedule 7 to the 1985 Act (important post-balance sheet events); and

    (d) the matters required by paragraph 6(b) of that Schedule (likely future developments in the business).

(2) The summary financial statement shall also contain the list of names of directors required by section 234(2) of the 1985 Act.

Summary profit and loss account: companies not required to prepare group accounts

3.—(l) The summary financial statement shall contain, in the case of a company the directors of which are not required to prepare group accounts for the financial year, a summary profit and loss account for the company, a summary consolidated profit and loss account, showing, in so far as they may be derived from the full profit and loss account, the items, listed in sub-paragraph (3) below, in the order set out in that sub-paragraph.

(2) The items or combination of items listed in sub-paragraph (3) below may appear under such headings as the directors consider appropriate.

(3) The items, or combination of items, referred to in sub-paragraph (1) above are—

    (a) interest receivable and payable:

the net figure resulting from the combination of the following two items–
—format 1, items 1 and 2
—format 2, items A1 and B1;

(b) dividend income, fees and commissions receivable and payable, dealing profits or losses and other operating income:
the net figure resulting from the combination of the following items–
—format 1, items 3, 4, 5, 6 and 7
—format 2, items, A2, A3, B2, B3, B4 and B7;

(c) administrative expenses, depreciation and amortisation, other operating charges, amounts written off, and adjustments to amounts written off, fixed asset investments:
the net figure resulting from the combination of the following items–
—format 1, items 8, 9, 10, 13 and 14
—format 2, items A4, A5, A6, A8 and B6;

(d) provisions and adjustments to provisions:
the net figure resulting from the combination of the following two items–
—format 1, items 11 and 12
—format 2, items A7 and B5;

(e) profit or loss on ordinary activities before tax:
—format 1, item 1
—format 2, item A9 or B8;

(f) tax on profit or loss on ordinary activities:
—format 1, item 16
—format 2, item A10;

(g) profit or loss on ordinary activities after tax:
—format 1, item 17
—format 2, item A11 or B9;

(h) extraordinary profit or loss after tax:
—format 1, item 22
—the net figure resulting from the combination of format 2, items A14 and B11;

(i)   other taxes not shown under the preceding items:
— format 1, item 23
— format 2, item A15;

(j)   profit or loss for the financial year:
— format 1, item 24
— format 2, items A16 or B12; and

(k)   the aggregate amount of dividends paid and, if not disclosed in the summary directors' report, proposed.

(4) The summary profit and loss account shall also show, at the end thereof and under such heading as the directors consider appropriate, the figure required by paragraph 1(1) of Part I of Schedule 6 to the 1985 Act (directors' emoluments).

Summary profit and loss account: companies required to prepare group accounts

4.—(1) The summary financial statement shall contain, in the case of a company the directors of which are required to prepare group accounts for the financial year, a summary consolidated profit and loss account showing the items, or combination of items, required by paragraph 3 above, in the order required by that paragraph and under such headings as the directors consider appropriate, but with the modifications specified in sub-paragraph (2) below.

(2) The modifications referred to in sub-paragraph (1) above are as follows–

(a)   between the information required by paragraph 3(3)(d) and that required by paragraph 3(3)(e) there shall in addition be shown, under such heading as the directors consider appropriate, the item "Income from associated undertakings" required to be shown in the Schedule 9 formats by paragraph 3(7)(ii) of Part II of Schedule 9 to the 1985 Act;

(b)   between the information required by paragraph 3(3)(g) and that required by paragraph 3(3)(h) there shall in addition be shown, under such heading as the directors consider appropriate, the item "Minority interests" required to be shown in the Schedule 9 formats by paragraph 17(3) of Schedule 4A to the 1985 Act as adapted by paragraph 3(3) of Part II of Schedule 9 to that Act; and

(c)   the figures required by paragraphs 3(3)(h) and (i) shall each be shown after the deduction or the addition (as the case may be) of the item "Minority interests" required to be shown in the Schedule 9 formats by paragraph 17(4) of Schedule 4A to the 1985 Act as adapted by paragraph 3(4) of Part II of Schedule 9 to that Act.

Summary balance sheet: companies not required to prepare group accounts

5.—(1) The summary financial statement shall contain, in the case of a company the directors of which are not required to prepare group accounts for the financial year, a summary balance sheet which shall show, in so far as they may be derived from the full balance sheet, the items, or combination of items, set out in sub-paragraph (2) below, in the order set out in that sub-paragraph and under such headings as the directors consider appropriate.

(2) The items, or combination of items, referred to in sub-paragraph (1) above are as follows–

(a)   cash and balances at central (or post office) banks, treasury bills and other eligible bills:
   —the aggregate of items 1 and 2 under the heading "ASSETS";

(b)   loans and advances to banks:
   —item 3 under the heading "ASSETS";

(c)   loans and advances to customers:
   —item 4 under the heading "ASSETS";

(d)   debt securities (and other fixed income securities), equity shares (and other variable-yield securities), participating interests and shares in group undertakings:
   —the aggregate of items 5, 6, 7 and 8 under the heading "ASSETS";

(e) intangible and tangible fixed assets:
—the aggregate of items 9 and 10 under the heading "ASSETS";

(f) called up capital not paid, own shares, other assets, pre-payments and accrued income:
—the aggregate of items 11 (or 14), 12, 13 and 15 under the heading "ASSETS";

(g) total assets under the heading "ASSETS";

(h) deposits by banks:
—item 1 under the heading "LIABILITIES";

(i) customer accounts:
—item 2 under the heading "LIABILITIES";

(j) debt securities in issue:
—item 3 under the heading "LIABILITIES";

(k) other liabilities, accruals and deferred income and provisions for liabilities and charges:
—the aggregate of terms 4, 5 and 6 under the heading "LIABILITIES";

(l) subordinated liabilities:
—item 7 under the heading "LIABILITIES";

(m) called up share capital, share premium account, reserves, revaluation reserve and profit and loss account:
—the aggregate of items 8, 9, 10, 11 and 12 under the heading "LIABILITIES";

(n) total liabilities under the heading "LIABILITIES";

(o) contingent liabilities:
—item 1 under the heading "MEMORANDUM ITEMS"; and

(p) commitments:
—item 2 under the heading "MEMORANDUM ITEMS".

Summary balance sheet: companies required to prepare group accounts

6.—(1) The summary financial statements shall contain, in the case of a company the directors of which are required to prepare group accounts, a summary consolidated balance sheet showing the items required by paragraph 5 above, in the order required by that paragraph and under such headings as the directors consider appropriate, but with the addition specified in sub-paragraph (2) below.

(2) Between the items required by paragraphs 5(2)(l) and (m) or after the item required by paragraph 5(2)(m) (whichever is the position adopted for the full accounts), there shall in addition be shown under an appropriate heading the item "Minority interests" required to be shown in the Schedule 9 format by paragraph 17(2) of Schedule 4A to the 1985 Act, as adapted by paragraph 3(2) of Part II of Schedule 9 to the 1985 Act.

Corresponding amounts

7. In respect of every item shown in the summary profit and loss account or summary consolidated profit and loss account (as the case may be), or in the summary balance sheet or summary consolidated balance sheet (as the case may be) the corresponding amount shall be shown for the immediately preceding financial year; for this purpose "the corresponding amount" is the amount shown in the summary financial statement for that year or which would have been so shown had such a statement been prepared for that year, after any adjustments necessary to ensure that that amount is comparable with the item for the financial year in question.

SCHEDULE 3

FORM AND CONTENT OF SUMMARY FINANCIAL STATEMENT OF INSURANCE COMPANIES OR GROUPS

Application of Schedule

1.—(1) Paragraphs 2 to 8 of this Schedule apply where the full annual accounts for the financial year have been prepared under

Part VII of the 1985 Act as amended by the Companies Act 1985 (Insurance Companies Accounts) Regulations 1993.

(2) Paragraphs 2 and 3 and 8 to 11 of this Schedule apply where the full annual accounts for the financial year have been prepared under the transitional arrangements (as defined in paragraph 9(1) of this Schedule).

(3) Paragraph 12 applies where the directors of a parent company of an insurance group, being entitled to do so, prepare group accounts for the financial year in an alternative form as permitted by article 7 of, and paragraph 3 of Part I of Schedule 2 to, the Companies Act 1989 (Commencement No. 4 and Transitional and Saving Provisions) Order 1990.

Form of summary financial statement

2.—(1) The summary financial statement shall contain the information prescribed by the following paragraphs of this Schedule, in such order and under such headings as the directors consider appropriate, together with any other information necessary to ensure that the summary financial statement is consistent with the full accounts and reports for the financial year in question.

(2) Nothing in this Schedule shall be construed as prohibiting the inclusion in the summary financial statement of any additional information derived from the company's annual accounts and directors' report.

Summary directors' report

3.—(1) The summary financial statement shall contain the whole of, or a summary of, that portion of the directors' report for the year in question which sets out the following matters—

    (a)   the matters required by section 234(1)(a) of the 1985 Act (business review);

    (b)   the amount recommended to be paid as dividend, if not disclosed in the summary profit and loss account;

(c) the matters required by paragraph 6(a) of Schedule 7 to the 1985 Act (important post-balance sheet events); and

(d) matters required by paragraph 6(b) of that Schedule (likely future developments in the business).

(2) The summary financial statement shall also contain the list of names of directors required by section 234(2) of the 1985 Act.

Summary profit and loss account: companies not required to prepare group accounts

4.—(1) The summary financial statement shall contain, in the case of a company the directors of which are not required to prepare group accounts for the financial year, a summary profit and loss account showing, in so far as they may be derived from the full profit and loss account, the items, or combinations of items, listed in sub-paragraph (3) below, in the order set out in that sub-paragraph.

(2) The items or combinations of items listed in sub-paragraph (3) below may appear under such headings as the directors consider appropriate.

(3) The items, or combinations of items, referred to in sub-paragraph (1) above are–

(a) gross premiums written—general business:
—item I 1(a);

(b) gross premiums written—long term business:
—item II 1(a);

(c) balance on the technical account for general business:
—item I 10;

(d) balance on the technical account for long term business:
—item II 13;

(e) other income and charges:
the net figure resulting from the combination of the following items–
—item III 3

—item III 3a
—item III 4
—item III 5
—item III 5a
—item III 6
—item III 7
—item III 8;

(f)   the profit or loss on ordinary activities before tax:
—item III 8a;

(g)   tax on profit or loss on ordinary activities:
—item III 9;

(h)   profit or loss on ordinary activities after tax:
—item III 10;

(i)   extraordinary profit or loss after tax:
—the net figure resulting from the combination of items III 13 and 14;

(j)   other taxes:
—item III 15;

(k)   profit or loss for the financial year:
—item III 16; and

(l)   the aggregate amount of dividends paid and, if not disclosed in the summary directors' report, proposed.

(4) The summary profit and loss account shall also show, at the end thereof and under such headings as the directors consider appropriate, the figure required by paragraph 1(1) of Part I of Schedule 6 to the 1985 Act (directors' emoluments).

Summary profit and loss account: companies required to prepare group accounts

5.—(1) The summary financial statement shall contain, in the case of a company the directors of which are required to prepare group accounts for the financial year, a summary consolidated profit and loss account showing the items, or combinations of items, required by paragraph 4 above, in the order required by that paragraph and under such headings as the directors consider appropriate, but with the modifications specified in sub-paragraph (2) below.

(2) The modifications referred to in sub-paragraph (1) above are as follows–

    (a)   between the information required by paragraph 4(3)(e) and that required by paragraph 4(3)(f) there shall in addition be shown, under such heading as the directors consider appropriate, the item "Income from associated undertakings" required to be shown in the Schedule 9A formats by paragraph 21(3)(b) of Schedule 4A to the 1985 Act, as adapted by paragraph 1(8) of Part II of Schedule 9A to that Act;

    (b)   between the information required by paragraph 4(3)(h) and that required by paragraph 4(3)(i) there shall in addition be shown, under such headings as the directors consider appropriate, the item "Minority interests" required to be shown in the Schedule 9A formats by paragraph 17(3) of Schedule 4A to the 1985 Act as adapted by paragraph 1(6)(c) of Part II of Schedule 9A to that Act; and

    (c)   the figures required by paragraph 4(3)(i) and (j) shall each be shown after the deduction or the addition (as the case may be) of the item "Minority interests" required to be shown in the Schedule 9A formats by paragraph 17(4) of Schedule 4A to the 1985 Act as adapted by paragraph 1(6)(d) of Part II of Schedule 9A to that Act.

Summary balance sheet: companies not required to prepare group accounts

6.—(1) The summary financial statement shall contain, in the case of a company the directors of which are not required to prepare group accounts for the financial year, a summary balance sheet which shall show, in so far as they may be derived from the full balance sheet, the items, or combinations of items, set out in sub-paragraph (2) below in the order of that sub-paragraph and under such headings as the directors consider appropriate.

(2) The items, or combinations of items, referred to in sub-paragraph (1) above are–

(a) investments:
—the aggregate of items C and D under the heading "ASSETS";

(b) reinsurers' share of technical provisions:
—item Da under the heading "ASSETS";

(c) other assets:
the aggregate of items A or E(IV), B, E(I) to (III), F and G under the heading "ASSETS";

(d) total assets under the heading "ASSETS";

(e) capital and reserves:
—item A under the heading "LIABILITIES";

(f) subordinated liabilities:
—item B under the heading "LIABILITIES";

(g) fund for future appropriations:
—item Ba under the heading "LIABILITIES";

(h) gross technical provisions:
—the aggregate of items C.1(a), C.2(a), C.3(a), C.4(a), C.5, C.6(a) and D(a) under the heading "LIABILITIES";

(i) technical provisions–reinsurance amounts:
—the aggregate of items C.1(b), C.2(b), C.3(b), C.4(b), C.6(b) and D(b) under the heading "LIABILITIES";

(j) other liabilities:
—the aggregate of items E, F, G and H under the heading "LIABILITIES"; and

(k) total liabilities under the heading "LIABILITIES".

Summary balance sheet: companies required to prepare group accounts

7.—(1) The summary financial statement shall contain, in the case of a company the directors of which are required to prepare group accounts for the financial year, a summary consolidated balance sheet which shall show the items required by paragraph 6 above, in the order required by that paragraph and under such headings as the directors consider appropriate, but with the addition of the item specified in sub-paragraph (2) below.

(2) Between the items required by paragraph 6(2)(d) and (e) above, there shall in addition be shown under an appropriate heading the item "Minority interests" required to be shown in the Schedule 9A format by paragraph 17(2) of Schedule 4A to the 1985 Act, as adapted by paragraph 1(6)(b) of Part II of Schedule 9A to the 1985 Act.

Corresponding amounts

8. In respect of every item shown in the summary profit and loss account or summary consolidated profit and loss account (as the case may be) or in the summary balance sheet or summary consolidated balance sheet (as the case may be) the corresponding amount shall be shown for the immediately preceding financial year; for this purpose "the corresponding amount" is the amount shown in the summary financial statement for that year or which would have been so shown had such a statement been prepared for that year, after any adjustments necessary to ensure that that amount is comparable with the item for the financial year in question.

Transitional arrangements: definition

9.—(1) In this Schedule "the transitional arrangements" means the transitional arrangements made by regulation 7 of the Companies Act 1985 (Insurance Companies Accounts) Regulations 1993 with respect to the amendments to the 1985 Act effected by regulations 2 to 5 of those Regulations (which allow annual accounts for a financial year commencing on a date prior to 23rd December 1994 to be prepared under the 1985 Act as in force prior to its amendment by those Regulations).

(2) Where the company is entitled to the exemptions conferred by paragraph 28 of Schedule 9A to the 1985 Act as continued in force under the transitional arrangements (the full accounts having been prepared under the transitional arrangements) and has relied upon them with respect to the full accounts from which the summary financial statement is to be drawn, the summary financial statement shall state that fact.

Summary profit and loss account under transitional arrangements

10.—(1) The summary financial statement shall contain, in the case of a company the directors of which are not required to prepare group accounts for the financial year, a summary profit and loss account, or, in the case of a company the directors of which are so required, a summary consolidated profit and loss account, showing, in so far as they may be derived from the full profit and loss account, amounts for the items set out in sub-paragraph (2) below under such headings as the directors consider appropriate.

(2) The items referred to in sub-paragraph (1) above are as follows–

(a) the profit or loss for the financial year before taxation;

(b) taxation, that is the combined amount of the charge to revenue for United Kingdom taxation required to be shown by paragraph 14(1)(c) of Schedule 9A to the 1985 Act and the charge for taxation imposed out of the United Kingdom on profits, income and (so far as charged to revenue) capital gains required to be shown by that paragraph;

(c) the profit or loss for the financial year after taxation;

(d) extraordinary and exceptional items, that is the amounts required by paragraph 18(6)(a) of the Schedule; and

(e) dividends paid and proposed, that is the aggregate amount of dividends paid and proposed required by paragraph 14(1)(k) of that Schedule.

(3) The summary profit and loss account shall also show, at the end thereof and under such heading as the directors consider appropriate, the figure required by paragraph 1(1) of Part I of Schedule 6 to the 1985 Act (directors' emoluments).

Summary balance sheet under transitional arrangements

11. The summary financial statement shall contain, in the case of a company the directors of which are not required to prepare group accounts for the financial year, a summary balance sheet or, in the case of a company the directors of which are so required, a summary consolidated balance sheet, which shall show, in so far as they may be derived from the full balance sheet, the following items–

(a) the amount of issued share capital required to be disclosed under paragraph 2 of Schedule 9A to the 1985 Act (issued share capital);

(b) an aggregate figure for the reserves required to be shown under paragraphs 4(1) and 7 of that Schedule (provisions);

(c) an aggregate figure for the provisions required to be shown under paragraphs 4(1) and 7 of that Schedule (provisions);

(d) an aggregate figure for liabilities required to be shown in the balance sheet under Part I of that Schedule (liabilities); and

(e) a combined figure for any assets required to be disclosed in the full balance sheet under the provisions of Part I of that Schedule (assets),

in each case under such headings as the directors consider appropriate.

Companies preparing alternative form group accounts

12. Where the directors of a parent company of an insurance group, being entitled to do so, prepare group accounts for the financial year in an alternative form,

(a) the summary financial statement for that company shall contain a summary profit and loss account for the group showing the information required by paragraph 10 above with such modifications as are required to summarise appropriately the profit or loss of the group;

(b) the summary financial statement for that company shall contain a summary balance sheet for the group showing the information required by paragraph 11 above with such modifications as are required to summarise appropriately the state of affairs of the group; and

(c) paragraph 8 above shall apply.

EXPLANATORY NOTE

(This note is not part of the Regulations)

These Regulations, which come into force on 1st September 1995, replace the Companies (Summary Financial Statement) Regulations 1992 (S.I.1992/3075) ("the 1992 Regulations").

The Regulations re-enact the provisions of the 1992 Regulations with minor and drafting amendments and with the following changes of substance–

(a) regulation 4 sets out the manner in which a listed public company is to ascertain whether an entitled person (as defined in regulation 2) wishes to receive a summary financial statement ("SFS") in place of the full accounts and reports for the financial year. If such companies have not received an express written notification from an entitled person, they can conduct a relevant consultation under regulation 6 of these Regulations (a procedure similar to that previously set out in regulation 6(3) of the 1992 Regulations). Alternatively, regulation 5 introduces a new procedure of sending entitled persons an advance notice describing what an SFS will contain and enclosing a reply-paid card on which entitled persons can indicate whether they wish to receive full accounts and reports;

(b) regulation 6(2)(b) of the 1992 Regulations (under which a failure by an entitled person to respond to a relevant consultation under that regulation impliedly counter-manded any previous notification of a wish to receive full accounts and reports) is not re-enacted in these Regulations;

(c) companies will only have to pay for the postage on cards sent to entitled persons under regulations 5(2) and 6(2)(d) of these Regulations if those persons have addresses in the European Economic Area (regulation 5(3) and 6(3));

(d) when an SFS is sent to an entitled person under the Regulations it will no longer be accompanied by a reply-paid card on which the entitled person can request full accounts and reports. The SFS will, however, contain a clear statement of the right of entitled persons to obtain a free copy of a company's full accounts and reports and of how that copy can be obtained, and of how they may elect to receive such accounts and reports rather than SFSs for future years (regulation 7(4) and(5));

(e) the revisions to the law on the content of the full statutory accounts of insurance companies and groups contained in the Companies Act 1985 (Insurance Companies Accounts) Regulations 1993 (S.I. 1993/3246) (and the transitional arrangements contained in those Regulations) are reflected in regulation 10 of, and Schedule 3 to, these Regulations;

(f) listed public companies other than insurance companies may continue to comply with the 1992 Regulations with respect to financial years commencing prior to 23rd December 1994 (regulation 11(2)). Special transitional arrangements for insurance companies are contained in Schedule 3; and

(g) the transitional provisions contained in paragraphs 3 and 7 of Schedule 2 to the 1992 Regulations are not re-enacted as they are spent.

Section 76 Building Societies Act 1986

76.—(1) The directors of a building society shall with respect to each financial year, prepare for members and depositors a summary financial statement for that year, that is to say, a statement derived from the annual accounts, annual business statement and directors report, giving a summary account of the society's financial development during and financial position at the end of the year.

(2) Where the society has *connected undertakings* the statement shall (so far as they are dealt with in the group accounts) give an account of the financial development and position of the society and its *connected undertakings*.

(3) The Commission may, by regulations made with the consent of the Treasury, make provision with respect to–

    (a)   the form of the summary financial statement and

    (b)   the information which must be included in it.

(4) Every summary financial statement shall also include in the prescribed form statements to the effect that–

    (a)   it is only a summary of information in the accounts, business statement and directors' report;

    (b)   in so far as it summarises the information in the accounts, those accounts have been audited;

    (c)   the accounts, business statement and directors' report will be available to members and depositors free of charge on demand at every office of the society after a specified date.

(5) Every summary financial statement shall include a statement of the auditors' opinion as to its consistency with the accounts, business statement and directors' report and its conformity with the requirements of this section and regulations made under it.

(6) The power to make regulations under subsection (3) above is exercisable by statutory instrument which shall be subject to annulment in pursuance of a resolution of either House of Parliament.

(7) The summary financial statement shall be signed by two directors on behalf of the board of directors and by the chief executive of the society.

(8) A copy of the summary financial statement and, where this subsection extends under section 78(6) to the auditors' report also, of the auditors' report shall be sent by the society, not later than 21 days before the date of the annual general meeting at which the accounts and reports are to be considered, to–

    (a)   every member of the society who is entitled to receive notice of the meeting,

    (b)   the Commission, and

    (c)   the central office.

(9) A copy of the summary financial statement and, where this subsection extends under section 78(6) to the auditors' report also, of the auditors' report shall be given or sent by the society free of charge, at any time during the period ending with the publication of the next summary financial statement, to–

    (a)   any individual who for the first time subscribes for shares in the society, on his first subscribing for the shares, and

    (b)   any member of the society who was not sent a copy under subsection (8)(a) above, within seven days of his making a demand for a copy.

(10) If default is made by a building society in complying with subsection (8) above, the society shall be liable on summary conviction–

    (a)   to a fine not exceeding level 5 on the standard scale; and

    (b)   in the case of a continuing offence, to an additional fine not exceeding £200 for every day during which the offence continues,

and so shall any officer who is also guilty of the offence.

(11) If default is made by a building society in complying with subsection (9) above, the society shall be liable on summary conviction–

(a) to a fine not exceeding level 3 on the standard scale and

(b) in the case of a continuing offence, to an additional fine not exceeding £40 for every day during which the offence continues,

and so shall any officer who is also guilty of the offence.

(12) The central office shall keep the copy of the summary financial statement received by it under subsection (8) above in the public file of the society.

Section 14 Companies (Revision of Defective Accounts and Report) Regulations 1990 (SI 1990 No 2570)

Summary financial statements

14.—(1) This Regulation has effect (subject to Regulation 16(3)) where the directors have prepared revised accounts or a revised report under section 245 of the Act and a summary financial statement based upon the original annual accounts or report has been sent to any person under section 251 of the Act.

(2) Where the summary financial statement would, if it had been prepared by reference to the revised accounts or revised report, not comply with the requirements of section 251 or the Companies (Summary Financial Statement) Regulations 1995 made thereunder, the directors of the company shall cause the company to prepare a further summary financial statement under section 251 and to send that statement to:

    (a)   any person who received a copy of the original summary financial statement; and

    (b)   to any person to whom the company would be entitled, as at the date the revised summary financial statement is prepared, to send a summary financial statement for the current financial year;

and section 251(1) to (4) and (7) shall apply *mutatis mutandis* to a financial statement hereunder.

(3) A summary financial statement prepared under the last paragraph shall contain a short statement of the revisions made and their effect.

(4) Where the summary financial statement would, if it had been prepared by reference to the revised accounts or revised report, comply with the requirements of section 251 and the Companies (Summary Financial Statement) Regulations 1995, the directors of the company shall cause the company to send to the persons referred to in paragraph (2) above a note stating that the annual

accounts of the company for the relevant financial year (specifying it) or (as the case may be) the directors' report for that year have or has been revised in a respect which has no bearing on the summary financial statement for that year.

If the auditors' report under Regulation 6 or 7 above on the revised accounts or revised report is qualified, a copy of that report shall be attached to the note sent out under this paragraph.

(5) A summary financial statement revised, or a note prepared, under this Regulation shall be sent to the persons referred to in paragraph (2) above within 28 days after the date of revision of the revised accounts or revised report.

(6) Section 251(6) of the Act shall apply with respect to a failure to comply with the requirements of this Regulation as if the provisions of this Regulation were provisions of section 251 and as if the reference therein to "the company and every officer of it who is in default" was a reference to each of the directors of the company who approved the revised accounts under Regulation 4 above or the revised report under Regulation 5 above.

Auditing guidance

The Auditors' Statement on the Summary Financial Statement

Preface

The purpose of this guidance is to clarify the auditors' responsibilities in connection with summary financial statements issued by listed companies under section 251[1] of the Companies Act 1985 and to describe how the principles of the Auditing Standard 'The audit report' should be applied to the auditors' statement on the summary financial statement.

1

All references are to the Companies Act 1985 ('the Act') as amended by the Companies Act 1989.

2

Background

Under section 238(1) of the Act a company is required to send to every member of the company copies of:

3

- the company's annual accounts:
- the directors' report for the financial year; and
- the auditors' report on those accounts.

However, section 251(1) states that:

4

'A public company whose shares, or any class of whose shares, are listed need not, in such cases as may be specified by regulations made by the Secretary of State, ... send copies of the documents referred to in section 238(1) to members of the company, but may instead send them a summary financial statement'.

For this purpose 'listed' means admitted to the Official List of The International Stock Exchange of the United Kingdom and the Republic of Ireland Limited.

---

[1] The equivalent legislation in Northern Ireland is contained in Article 259 of the Companies (Northern Ireland) Order 1986. There is no equivalent legislation in the Republic of Ireland.

5 The summary financial statement must be derived from the annual accounts and directors' report, and must explicitly follow the detailed requirements concerning its form and content which are set out in The Companies (Summary Financial Statement) Regulations 1990 (SI 1990/515),[2] referred to in this guideline as 'the Regulations' (section 251(3)).

6 Section 251(4) specifies that the summary financial statement shall:

'(a) state that it is only a summary of information in the company's annual accounts and the directors' report;

(b) contain a statement by the company's auditors of their opinion as to whether the summary financial statement is consistent with those accounts and that report and complies with the requirements of this section and regulations made under it;

(c) state whether the auditors' report on the annual accounts was unqualified or qualified, and if it was qualified set out the report in full together with any further material needed to understand the qualification;

(d) state whether the auditors' report on the annual accounts contained a statement under:

(i) section 237(2) (accounting records or returns inadequate or accounts not agreeing with the records and returns), or

(ii) section 237(3) (failure to obtain necessary information and explanations),

and if so, set out the statement in full.'

The auditors' procedures

7 The summary financial statement must contain a statement of the auditors' opinion on the matters specified in section 251(4)(b) (see paragraph 6 above). Therefore, when planning the audit of the annual accounts of a listed company, the auditors should ascertain

---

[2] The equivalent regulations in Northern Ireland are contained in The Companies (Summary Financial Statement) Regulations Northern Ireland 1990 (SR 378 of 1990).

whether a summary financial statement will be prepared. Where applicable, the auditors' engagement letter should refer to their responsibilities in relation to the summary financial statement (see the Auditing Guideline 'Engagement letters'). It will usually be desirable for the auditors to carry out their work on the summary financial statement at the same time as, rather than after, completing the audit, so that their statement under section 251(4)(b) and their audit report can be issued at the same time. The auditors should therefore encourage the directors to take this into account when they are planning the timetable for the preparation of the annual accounts.

The auditors' procedures in relation to the summary financial **8** statement will be directed towards consideration of the matters on which they are required, by section 251(4)(b), to express an opinion, namely:

- whether it is consistent with the annual accounts and the directors' report; and
- whether it complies with the requirements of section 251 and of the Regulations.

It should be noted, however, that these opinions are not independent of each other; it is a requirement of the Regulations that the summary financial statement includes not only the detailed information specifically prescribed by the Regulations but also any other information necessary to ensure that it is consistent with the annual accounts and directors' report (see paragraph 1(2) of Schedules 1 and 2 to the Regulations).

CONSISTENCY

The auditors are required to state whether in their opinion the **9** summary financial statement is consistent with the annual accounts and the directors' report. The auditors are not required to form an opinion on whether the summary financial statement gives a true and fair view.

It is in any event most unlikely that the summary financial state- **10** ment could give a true and fair view in any practical situation, as much of the detailed information from which it has been extracted is not presented. The summary financial statement is required (by section 251(4)(a)) to include a statement that it is only a summary and also (by the Regulations) to include in a prominent position a statement that it does not contain sufficient information to allow for a full understanding of the company's results and its state of affairs.

11 In order to be satisfied that the summary financial statement is consistent with the annual accounts and directors' report, the auditors will not merely be concerned with whether the detailed information required by the Regulations has been properly extracted and transferred to the summary financial statement. They should also consider whether the summary financial statement needs to contain any other information (i.e. in addition to that specifically prescribed) in order to ensure that it is consistent with the annual accounts and directors' report.

12 Matters which may give rise to an inconsistency include:

- information which has been inaccurately extracted from the annual accounts and directors' report (for example, incorrect classification of balance sheet items);
- information which, in the auditors' opinion, has been summarised in a manner which is not consistent with the annual accounts and directors' report (for example, unduly selective summarisation of the directors' report); and
- omission from the summary financial statement of information which is not specifically required by the Regulations but which, in the auditors' opinion, is necessary to ensure consistency with the annual accounts and directors' report (for example, omission of information relating to an exceptional item or a non-adjusting post balance sheet event which the auditors consider fundamental to a shareholder's understanding of the company's results or financial position).

13 When the auditors identify what they believe may be an inconsistency they should discuss the matter with the directors or senior management, as appropriate, so that they may eliminate the inconsistency, for example by including additional information in

the summary financial statement or by making appropriate amendments to the annual accounts or directors' report.

If discussion with the directors or senior management does not **14** result in the elimination of the inconsistency, the auditors should qualify their statement under section 251(4)(b). The qualified statement should include a description of the inconsistency (see also paragraph 19 below).

COMPLIANCE WITH SECTION 251 AND THE REGULATIONS

In order to give the statement of opinion required by section **15** 251(4)(b) the auditors will need to give consideration to the specific and detailed requirements of section 251 and the Regulations.

Section 251(3) states that the summary financial statement shall be **16** derived from the annual accounts and directors' report. The auditors will therefore need to consider whether the summary financial statement contains any material which, although it is not inconsistent with the annual accounts and directors' report, is nevertheless not properly derived from them in the manner specified by the Regulations.

If the auditors' report on the annual accounts was qualified, or if it **17** included a statement under section 237(2) or (3), the auditors will need to consider whether the qualified report or statement is accurately reproduced in the summary financial statement, as required by section 251(4)(c) and (d). They should also consider whether a reader of the summary financial statement will be able to understand the circumstances giving rise to the qualified audit report or statement. Usually the requirement to reproduce in the summary financial statement the full text of the qualified report or statement will ensure this. But section 251(4)(c) requires that any further material needed to understand the qualified report should also be set out. Therefore, where the qualification includes a reference to a note to the annual accounts but does not explicitly state all the relevant information contained in that note, such information should also be reproduced in the summary financial statement.

18 The auditors should satisfy themselves that the other items required by section 251 and the Regulations (such as the statements referred to in paragraph 10 above) are also included in the summary financial statement.

19 An inconsistency between the summary financial statement and the annual accounts and directors' report will also mean that the summary financial statement is not properly derived from them and does not comply with the Regulations; it will therefore lead to a qualification of the auditors' statement on the grounds of non-compliance with section 251 and the Regulations as well as on the grounds of the inconsistency.

OTHER CONSIDERATIONS

20 The summary financial statement may be issued as part of some other form of communication to members of the company, such as a newsletter. Where this occurs, the summary financial statement should form a separate and clearly identified part of the larger document. The auditors' statement on the summary financial statement will refer only to the summary financial statement and not to any other material included in the same document. However, the auditors should ensure that they are not associated with any information which could be misleading. They should therefore urge the directors not to issue any document containing the summary financial statement until they have had an opportunity to read the other material which will be included with it. The auditors should make arrangements to see, prior to publication, any document in which the summary financial statement is to be included. If they disagree with any of this material they should discuss the matter with the directors. If the amendments the auditors consider necessary are not made, they should consider taking legal advice.

The auditors' statement

21 The auditors' statement on the summary financial statement will incorporate the following elements:

The Auditors' Statement on the Summary Financial Statement

- Addressee – the Act does not specify that the auditors' statement should be addressed; in the absence of any other requirement it should be addressed to the members of the company.
- Scope of statement – the summary financial statement should be clearly identified.
- Opinion – the auditors should express their opinion as to whether the summary financial statement is consistent with the annual accounts and the directors' report and whether it complies with the requirements of section 251 and the regulations made under it.
- Date – the auditors' statement should be dated on or as soon as possible after the date of their audit report on the annual accounts (see paragraph 7 above). In any event it cannot be dated before the date of that report or before the date on which the summary financial statement is approved by the board of directors.

An example of such a statement is given in the Appendix to this guideline. If the auditors cannot give the opinion indicated above, they should qualify their statement in accordance with the Auditing Standard 'The audit report'.

Appendix – Example of a statement on the summary financial statement

AUDITORS' STATEMENT TO THE MEMBERS OF XYZ PUBLIC LIMITED COMPANY

In our opinion the summary financial statement above/overleaf is consistent with the annual accounts and directors' report of XYZ Public Limited Company for the year ended 31 December 19..... and complies with the requirements of section 251 of the Companies Act 1985 and the regulations made thereunder.

Auditors

Date

Extracts from published summary financial statements

PILKINGTON

Pilkington: financial highlights

At constant exchange rates		1998/1999 At constant exchange rates £m	1998/1999 As reported £m	1997/1998 £m
Down 8%	Turnover	2,752	2,709	2,991
Up 20%	Operating profit	223	214	186
Up 28%	Pre-tax profit	154	135	120
Up 90%	Earnings per share	7.8p	6.5p	4.1p

We promised to make the business simpler.
We have created a simpler organisation, based on business lines. The Group's central functions are applying common standards across the business, securing substantial cost reductions.

simpler

more focused

We said we would review the strategy of our Building Products business in Europe.
The business has been radically restructured. Last year it achieved good profitability, meeting our initial financial targets.

We said we must drive for manufacturing excellence at lowest cost.
Productivity in our float glass plants is more than 30 per cent higher than two years ago; in our Automotive Products original equipment business, it is more than 25 per cent higher.

more efficient

lower cost

We promised to reduce overhead costs.
Over the last two years we have cut our overhead costs by £160 million. We aim to reduce them on a like-for-like basis by at least a further £30 million a year.

135

NATWEST

NatWest: summary accounts

Summary consolidated profit and loss account
for the year ended 31 December 1998

	Notes	1998 £m	1997[I] £m
Net interest income[II]		**3,811**	3,664
Non-interest income		**3,556**	3,310
Operating income		**7,367**	6,974
Operating expenses	1	**(5,055)**	(5,274)
Trading surplus		**2,312**	1,700
Provisions for bad and doubtful debts	2	**(499)**	(562)
Provisions for contingent liabilities and commitments		**–**	(5)
Amounts written off fixed asset investments		**(28)**	(31)
Operating profit		**1,785**	1,102
Income from associated undertakings		**29**	13
Disposal of tangible fixed assets		**(21)**	25
Losses on closure of Equities operations		**–**	(287)
Profit on sale of businesses	3	**265**	43
Profit on continuing operations		**2,058**	896
Discontinued operations			
Additional consideration on sale of Bancorp		**84**	79
Profit on ordinary activities before tax	4	**2,142**	975
Tax on profit on ordinary activities[II]	5	**(501)**	(309)
Profit on ordinary activities after tax		**1,641**	666
Minority interests – equity		**(24)**	(30)
Profit for the financial year		**1,617**	636
Preference dividends – non-equity		**(51)**	(45)
Ordinary dividends	6	**(613)**	(557)
		(664)	(602)
Retention for the year		**953**	34

I Restated following implementation of Financial Reporting Standard 10 'Goodwill and Intangible Assets' (see note 1, page 27).
II Net interest income is after a charge for finance leases of £55 million (1997: £106 million) following the change in the rate of UK corporation tax. A corresponding release of deferred tax has been credited to the tax charge for each year.

The total emoluments of directors who served in the year were £4,850,000 (1997: £3,948,000) and retirement benefits are accruing to 5 directors (1997: 5) under defined benefit pension schemes of the Group (see page 22).

Marginal glossary notes

A Provisions for bad and doubtful debts
The amount we take off our profit to allow for customers who cannot, or might not be able to, repay the money they owe us.

B Minority interests
The interests of other people who hold shares in our subsidiary companies.

C Retention for the year
The result for the year (after taking off tax, minority interests and dividends) transferred to reserves.

D Earnings per ordinary share – basic
Our profit for the financial year (less preference dividends) divided by the number of ordinary shares worked out to have been in issue during the year. Earnings per ordinary share is usually given in pence for each share.

E Earnings per ordinary share – diluted
The reduced earnings per ordinary share (see above) that results from including the new shares we would need to issue to meet the share options we have granted.

F Net asset value per ordinary share
Our ordinary share capital plus reserves, divided by the number of ordinary shares in issue at the end of the year. The net asset value is usually given in pence for each share.

Information per ordinary share

	Note	1998 pence	1997[I] pence
Dividends – net		**36.0**	32.2
Earnings – basic	7	**91.2**	34.5
Earnings – diluted	7	**90.1**	33.9
Earnings – headline	7	**78.1**	46.9
Net asset value		**471**	425

I Restated following implementation of Financial Reporting Standard 10 'Goodwill and Intangible Assets' (see note 1, page 27).

Statement of consolidated total recognised gains and losses
for the year ended 31 December 1998

	1998 £m	1997[I] £m
Profit for the financial year	**1,617**	636
Other recognised gains and (losses)		
Revaluation of freehold properties	**40**	32
Exchange and other movements	**5**	(67)
	45	(35)
Total recognised gains for the year	**1,662**	601
Prior year adjustment – cumulative goodwill amortisation	**(188)**	
Total recognised gains since 31 December 1997	**1,474**	

I Restated following implementation of Financial Reporting Standard 10 'Goodwill and Intangible Assets' (see note 1, page 27).

Summary consolidated balance sheet of the NatWest Group
at 31 December 1998

	1998 £m	1997[1] £m
Assets		
Cash and balances at central banks	1,055	905
Items in the course of collection from other banks	2,433	2,599
Treasury and other eligible bills	5,859	6,246
Loans and advances to banks	32,369	32,016
Loans and advances to customers	78,962	84,475
Operating lease assets	1,308	1,703
Debt securities and equity shares	37,896	34,761
A Interests in associated undertakings	93	67
B Intangible fixed assets	639	739
C Tangible fixed assets	2,454	2,761
D Other assets, prepayments and accrued income	15,706	15,622
	178,774	181,894
Long-term assurance assets attributable to policyholders	7,219	3,600
Total assets	185,993	185,494
Liabilities		
Items in the course of transmission to other banks	1,268	1,320
Deposits by banks	26,562	28,102
Customer accounts	96,294	89,888
Debt securities in issue	15,555	17,797
E Other liabilities, accruals, deferred income and provisions	25,285	31,480
Subordinated liabilities	5,162	5,145
Minority interests including non-equity interests	147	175
Called up share capital	1,705	1,731
Ordinary shares	472	623
Preference shares	1,181	1,105
Share premium account	259	75
Other reserves	23	(56)
Revaluation reserve	4,861	4,509
Profit and loss account		
F Shareholders' funds including non-equity interests	8,501	7,987
	178,774	181,894
Long-term assurance liabilities attributable to policyholders	7,219	3,600
Total liabilities	185,993	185,494
Memorandum items		
G Contingent liabilities	10,785	10,576
Commitments	48,164	53,333

1 Restated following implementation of Financial Reporting Standard 10 'Goodwill and Intangible Assets' (see note 1, page 27).

This summary financial statement was approved by the Board of directors on 22 February 1999 and signed on its behalf by

Robert Alexander
Chairman

Derek Wanless
Group Chief Executive

Richard Delbridge
Group Chief Financial Officer

A **Associated undertakings**
Businesses in which we own a significant percentage of the shares. We influence their policies but we do not control them.

B **Intangible fixed assets**
Amounts recognised as goodwill on our balance sheet.

C **Tangible fixed assets**
Property, machinery, equipment and similar items which we own and use to run our business.

D **Other assets, prepayments and accrued income**
Assets which cannot be included under any other asset heading on the balance sheet together with payments we have already made relating to future periods and income we have earned but not yet received.

E **Other liabilities, accruals, deferred income and provisions**
These are items which cannot be included in any other liability heading on the balance sheet. It also includes money we owe for goods and services, income received in advance and amounts set aside for liabilities that are not yet certain.

F **Shareholders' funds**
Shareholders' funds including non-equity interests is the total of ordinary shareholders' funds and preference share capital.

G **Contingent liabilities**
Debts or obligations which may come about if a particular event happens in the future.

Extracts from published summary financial statements

Summary consolidated cash flow statement
for the year ended 31 December 1998

	1998 £m	1997[I] £m
Net cash inflow/(outflow) from operating activities	**5,221**	(320)
Net cash outflow from returns on investments and servicing of finance	**(474)**	(454)
Taxation	**(314)**	(288)
Net cash outflow from capital expenditure and financial investment	**(4,793)**	(421)
Net cash inflow from acquisitions and disposals	**1,825**	141
Equity dividends paid	**(575)**	(488)
Net cash inflow/(outflow) before financing	**890**	(1,830)
Net cash (outflow)/inflow from financing	**(419)**	718
Increase/(decrease) in cash	**471**	(1,112)
Reconciliation of operating profit to net cash inflow/(outflow) from operating activities		
Operating profit	**1,785**	1,102
(Increase)/decrease in accrued income	**(153)**	18
Interest on subordinated liabilities	**386**	379
(Decrease)/increase in accruals and deferred income	**(7)**	413
Provisions for bad and doubtful debts	**499**	562
Loans and advances written off net of recoveries	**(420)**	(613)
Depreciation and amortisation of tangible and intangible fixed assets	**361**	359
Depreciation of operating lease assets	**366**	336
Other non-cash movements	**(348)**	(290)
Net cash inflow from trading activities	**2,469**	2,266
Decrease in items in the course of collection	**166**	213
Decrease/(increase) in treasury and other eligible bills	**327**	(1,201)
(Increase)/decrease in loans and advances to banks	**(1,473)**	2,153
Decrease/(increase) in loans and advances to customers	**1,503**	(3,129)
(Increase)/decrease in securities	**(1,940)**	1,615
Increase in other assets	**(225)**	(191)
Decrease in items in the course of transmission	**(52)**	(354)
Increase/(decrease) in deposits by banks	**2,027**	(8,215)
Increase in customer accounts	**6,960**	5,742
Decrease in debt securities in issue	**(2,129)**	(617)
(Decrease)/increase in other liabilities	**(2,277)**	1,182
Effect of accruals, deferrals and other non-cash movements	**(135)**	216
Net cash inflow/(outflow) from operating activities	**5,221**	(320)

I Restated following implementation of Financial Reporting Standard 10 'Goodwill and Intangible Assets' (see note 1, page 27).

Reconciliation of movements in consolidated shareholders' funds
for the year ended 31 December 1998

	Notes	1998 £m	1997[I] £m
Profit for the financial year		**1,617**	636
Dividends		**(664)**	(602)
Retention for the year		**953**	34
Other recognised gains and (losses)		**45**	(35)
Issue of shares, net of expenses		**42**	257
Repurchase of ordinary shares		**(375)**	–
Redemption of preference shares		**(147)**	–
Exchange movement on preference shares		**(4)**	5
Net increase in shareholders' funds		**514**	261
Opening shareholders' funds as previously reported		**7,897**	7,552
Prior year adjustment	1	**90**	174
Opening shareholders' funds as restated		**7,987**	7,726
Closing shareholders' funds		**8,501**	7,987

I Restated following implementation of Financial Reporting Standard 10 'Goodwill and Intangible Assets' (see note 1, page 27).

Notes to the summary financial statement
for the year ended 31 December 1998

1 Accounting policies
The Group's accounting policy for goodwill has been changed in line with Financial Reporting Standard 10 'Goodwill and Intangible Assets'. Purchased goodwill is capitalised, classified as an asset and amortised over its useful economic life. The gain or loss on the disposal of a subsidiary or associated undertaking is calculated by comparing the carrying value of the net assets sold (including any unamortised goodwill) with the proceeds received. Previously the Group's policy was for goodwill to be either deducted from profit and loss account reserves or capitalised. Goodwill eliminated from reserves in prior periods has been reinstated by means of a prior year adjustment and comparatives restated. The effects of this change of policy has been to increase the Group's profit before tax by £29 million in 1998 and decrease profit by £36 million in 1997, while increasing intangible assets and shareholders' funds by £38 million at 31 December 1998 and £90 million at 31 December 1997. There have been no other changes to the Group's principal accounting policies in the year.

2 Provisions for bad and doubtful debts
Provisions for bad and doubtful debts at 31 December 1998 amounted to £1,372 million (1997 £1,402 million) of which £965 million (1997 £1,005 million) is specific and £407 million (1997 £397 million) is general.

3 Profit on sale of businesses
This comprised mainly profits on disposal of Lombard point of sale businesses, Lex Vehicle Leasing, Cash and Equity Derivatives businesses, Coutts Bahamas and Institutional Trust businesses. These profits were partially offset by losses on disposal of the Australian trading operations. In 1997 the profits were realised from the sale of County NatWest Investment Management Australia Limited and McLean Budden Limited of Canada.

4 Profit/(loss) on ordinary activities before tax by business segment	1998 £m	1997[I] £m
NatWest UK[II]	1,058	1,012
Lombard	372	192
Ulster Bank Group	155	144
NatWest Wealth Management	360	193
Global Financial Markets[II]	393	244
Greenwich NatWest[III]	(98)	(687)
Other Businesses[III]	(79)	(53)
Head Office costs and other central items[IV]	(103)	(149)
Profit before tax – continuing operations	2,058	896
Profit on disposal of discontinued operations – Bancorp	84	79
	2,142	975

I Restated following implementation of Financial Reporting Standard 10 'Goodwill and Intangible Assets' (see note 1, above).
II From 1 January 1998, we changed the way we reward NatWest UK for business introduced to Global Financial Markets. The 1997 figures have been restated, increasing NatWest UK's 1997 income by £50 million and reducing Global Financial Markets' income by a similar amount.
III Corporate Advisory which was previously included in Greenwich NatWest is now included in Other Businesses.
IV Including £80 million general provision in 1997 for South East Asia and South Korea which is held centrally.

5 Tax on profit on ordinary activities
The tax charge for the year at £501 million, equivalent to 23.4% of pre-tax profit, benefited from a release of deferred tax of £59 million, resulting from the reduction in the rate of Corporation Tax from 31% to 30% enacted by the Finance Act 1998 with effect from 1 April 1999. Utilisation of capital losses and rollover relief led to only a small tax charge on disposal of subsidiaries, including the second tranche of the additional consideration received on the sale of Bancorp. Excluding these items, the underlying tax rate was 29.5% (1997 35.5%). This was lower than the 1998 effective UK Corporation Tax rate of 31.0% largely due to non-taxable income and overseas income taxed at lower rates being only partially offset by overseas losses for which no relief is currently available, overseas profits taxed at higher rates and other items, mainly goodwill amortisation, which are not allowable for tax purposes.

The UK Corporation Tax charge includes notional tax of £23 million (1997 £25 million) on the shareholders' interest in the increase in value of the Group's long-term assurance business.

6 Ordinary dividends	1998		1997	
	pence per share	£m	pence per share	£m
Interim (paid)	11.8	201	10.6	181
Final	24.2	412	21.6	376
	36.0	613	32.2	557

7 Earnings per ordinary share
Basic earnings per ordinary share are calculated by dividing the Group profit attributable to ordinary shareholders, of £1,566 million (1997 £591 million restated see note 1) by the weighted average number of ordinary shares in issue during the year of 1,717 million (1997 1,716 million). Diluted earnings per share are calculated based on the same profit and a weighted average number of shares of 1,739 million (1997 1,741 million).

Headline earnings, as defined by the Institute of Investment Management and Research, are calculated by adjusting the profit attributable to ordinary shareholders, for the after-tax profits or losses on sales or closures of businesses and tangible fixed assets, impairment of tangible fixed assets and goodwill amortisation, giving headline earnings of £1,341 million (1997 £805 million restated see note 1).

8 Litigation
Members of the Group are engaged in litigation in the United Kingdom and a number of overseas jurisdictions, including the United States, involving claims by and against them which arise in the ordinary course of business. The directors of the Bank, after reviewing the claims pending and threatened against Group undertakings and taking into account the advice of the relevant legal advisers, are satisfied that the outcome of these claims will not have a material adverse effect on the net assets of the Group.

ORANGE

Extracts from published summary financial statements

Orange: summary remuneration report

The full Remuneration Report can be found in the 1998 Annual Report/Form 20-F (to order a copy see page 30). The following extracts provide information on the directors' emoluments and interests in shares and options over the Company's shares.

Emoluments
Executive directors

	Hans Snook		Graham Howe		Colin Tucker		Total	
	1998 £000	1997 £000	1998 £000	1997 £000	1998 £000	1997 £000	1998 £000	1997 £000
Basic salary	503	457	256	238	190	180	949	875
Benefits	36	38	19	18	15	13	70	69
Performance related bonus	241	321	123	167	91	126	455	614
Pension contributions	–	–	41	38	30	29	71	67
	780	816	439	461	326	348	1,545	1,625

Basic salary
Salaries are determined by the Remuneration Committee and are reviewed annually having regard to Group results for the previous year, individual performance and market rates.

Benefits
Benefits include a car, fuel benefit, healthcare, life assurance and disablement and medical insurances.

Performance related bonuses
The annual bonus plan is based on agreed financial targets linked to the performance of the Group. A bonus of 60% of basic salary applies where these targets are achieved and the maximum possible bonus is 75% of basic salary.

Pensions
A defined contribution (money purchase) pension scheme is operated for all staff, including executive directors with the exception of Hans Snook who, under separate contractual arrangements with Hutchison Whampoa, remains a member of the Hutchison Whampoa scheme.

Non-executive directors

	John Bond		Don Fullerton		Richard Lapthorne		Paul Myners		George Rose		Total	
	1998 £000	1997 £000	1998 £000	1997 £000	1998 £000	1997 £000	1998 £000	1997 £000	1998 £000	1997 £000	1998 £000	1997 £000
Fees	25	25	25	25	16	–	25	25	16	–	107	75

The fees received by Messrs Rose and Lapthorne relate to the eight month period from their reappointment to the Board on 8 May 1998 to 31 December 1998. The non-executive directors appointed by Hutchison Whampoa do not receive fees.

Long term rewards
Share option schemes
Executive share options are considered important for market related retention and motivational purposes. Option grants are made on an annual basis to executives at the discretion of the Remuneration Committee. These grants are subject to a performance condition and an individual maximum of four times basic salary for directors. The aim is to relate the ability to exercise options with sustained improvements in the underlying financial performance of the Group.

The executive directors also participate in an all-employee savings related share option scheme.

Long term incentive plan
The long term incentive plan has been established for executive directors and certain senior employees. It is a share based scheme where the receipt of shares is linked to the Company's total shareholder return (TSR) ranked against other FTSE-100 companies. Participants receive shares on the expiry of the performance period, which will normally be the third anniversary of the award being made, provided the plan's performance condition set by the Remuneration Committee has been satisfied.

The number of shares received on the vesting of an award will depend on the extent to which the plan's performance condition has been satisfied. In order to receive the minimum award of 10% of the shares, the Remuneration Committee must be satisfied that the TSR in relation to the Company over the performance period, when compared to the TSR of the companies in the FTSE-100 over the same period, places it in the top 60 companies. All the shares comprised in the award will vest if the Company is placed in the top 25 companies. For these purposes TSR will be measured by reference to the movement in share price and the value of any dividends paid.

Directors' interests in share options and long term incentive plan awards
No options or awards lapsed, vested or were exercised during the year and the cumulative position at 31 December was as follows:

	LTIP Awards 1998	LTIP Awards 1997	Executive Options 1998	Executive Options 1997	Sharesave Options 1998	Sharesave Options 1997
Hans Snook	324,867	245,862	800,669	603,077	9,175	9,175
Graham Howe	171,641	131,432	415,133	324,557	9,175	9,175
Colin Tucker	114,570	84,728	287,076	196,107	9,175	9,175

None of the benefits from long term rewards are pensionable.

Directors' interests in shares

	Shares 1998	Shares 1997		Shares 1998	Shares 1997
Canning Fok	24,390	24,390	Lord Derwent	9,878	9,878
Hans Snook	50,000	50,000	Don Fullerton	9,756	9,756
Graham Howe	25,000	25,000	Richard Lapthorne	9,756	9,756
Colin Tucker	975	975	Paul Myners	50,000	50,000
John Bond	9,756	9,756	George Rose	4,878	4,878
Susan Chow	14,634	14,634	Frank Sixt	–	–

All shares are beneficially held. John Bond has a beneficial interest in £100,000 of the Orange 8.625% Senior Notes due 2008. There were no changes in the interests of the directors between 31 December 1998 and 24 February 1999.

BRADFORD AND BINGLEY

Extracts from published summary financial statements

Bradford and Bingley: 1998 summary financial statement

Summary financial statement

Bradford & Bingley Building Society Summary Financial Statement for the year ended 31st December 1998.

This financial statement is a summary of information in the audited annual accounts, the directors' report and annual business statement, all of which will be available to members and depositors free of charge on request at every office of Bradford & Bingley Building Society from 5th April 1999.

It was approved by the Board of Directors on 23rd February 1999 and signed on their behalf by:

J. Lindsay Mackinlay	Chairman
D. Trevor Lewis	Vice-Chairman
Christopher J. Rodrigues	Group Chief Executive

1998 was a great year

- We returned, on average, £2 million per week to members in the form of better mortgage and savings rates.
- We grew faster than the market due to consistently competitive rates.
- Lending to members for home ownership increased by £1,015 million.
- We retained our position as the UK's largest high street independent financial adviser and grew our financial planning business by 19%.
- Over 300,000 of our customers have now benefited from a free financial review.
- With the acquisition of Black Horse Agencies we expanded our network by 370 branches and are now on almost 1,000 high streets across the UK.
- We achieved all this while:
  - Management expenses reduced as a percentage of mean assets under management from 1.11 to 1.07 (excluding exceptional items and Black Horse Agencies).
  - Profits increased by 33% to £84 million (1997: £63 million).
  - General reserves increased to £1,050 million (1997: £966 million). Annual profits are added to reserves and support the continued growth of the Group.
  - Assets under management grew to £22.2 billion (1997: £19.7 billion).

Summary Directors' report

Our strong financial performance was achieved without compromising our commitment to the principles of a building society. As in previous years, we continued the policy of giving members real benefits in the form of better rates and services.

Larger network

A major event in 1998 was the acquisition of Black Horse Agencies from Lloyds TSB, adding the country's fourth largest estate agency and a leading property services business to Bradford & Bingley Group activities. The purchase also increased Bradford & Bingley's high street network by 370 branches, taking our national presence to almost 1,000 including building society branches and local agents.

Independent Financial Advice

Bradford & Bingley remained the largest high street provider of Independent Financial Advice (IFA) and our financial planning business increased by 19%. Our professional advisers give impartial advice on pensions, life insurance and investments. During 1998 we welcomed over 40,000 new customers for a financial review.

By mid-1999 we will have 150 more independent financial advisers in our estate agency branches, taking the total for the Group to over 500.

Better savings rates

Our branch based instant access and notice savings accounts provided consistently better rates than banks and converted building societies.

Our Tessa account was the first to pay 8% interest during 1998 and regularly featured in the best buy tables, attracting over 100,000 new Tessa customers.

Over 200,000 member families have taken advantage of our KidZone savings account, receiving exclusive free Puffin and Penguin books, as well as an excellent rate.

Existing members were offered the exclusive Loyalty Bond with a guaranteed interest rate of 7.5% until 31st March 1999.

Mortgages

Our standard variable rate remains among the lowest in the market and we offer a highly competitive range of fixed, capped and discount mortgage products. Our highly rated mortgage advisers have served a record number of customers, and received industry recognition.

The Group is also a leading provider of long-term finance to the housing association movement - non-profit organisations that provide affordable rented housing for those in need. Over 30,000 council homes throughout the UK have been purchased and refurbished thanks to our loan packages. In 1998 our total loan commitment to housing associations reached £1 billion.

Supporting the community

Last year we spent £500,000 providing help and support to the community. We assisted almost 100 local charities and community causes in 1998. From the lifeboat fund in Lerwick, to training volunteer staff to help children learn to read in Bingley, we continue to support a wide range of excellent causes.

This funding included the secondment of a number of managers and staff to charities and community initiatives with the support of Business in the Community, providing a valuable resource to numerous organisations.

Year 2000

We have been reviewing all business systems for year 2000 compliance and amending them accordingly. We are confident that our customers will suffer no ill effects when the calendar changes.

Mutuality debate

At the end of 1998 we received a resolution, put by a small number of members, asking the Board to consider taking steps to convert from a building society to a PLC. The Board is strongly opposed to this resolution. We believe our performance during 1998 demonstrates that mutuality is a winning formula.

Results for the year (£m)

	1998	1997
Net interest receivable	275	225
Other income and charges	163	84
Administrative expenses	(313)	(217)
Operating profit before provisions	125	92
Provisions	4	2
Profit for the year before taxation	129	94
Taxation	(45)	(31)
Profit for the year	84	63

Financial position at the end of the year (£m)

	1998	1997
Assets		
Liquid assets	4,352	3,280
Mortgages	16,505	15,040
Other loans	37	44
Fixed and other assets	515	391
Total assets	21,409	18,755
Liabilities		
Shares	12,838	11,259
Borrowings	6,684	5,886
Other liabilities	377	304
Subordinated liabilities	350	230
Subscribed capital	110	110
Reserves	1,050	966
Total liabilities	21,409	18,755

Summary of key financial ratios (%) and accompanying notes

	1998	1997
Gross capital as a percentage of shares and borrowings	7.73	7.62
Liquid assets as a percentage of shares and borrowings	22.29	19.13
Profit for the year as a percentage of mean total assets	0.42	0.35
Management expenses as a percentage of mean total assets	1.56	1.21
Management expenses as a percentage of mean managed total assets (excluding exceptional items and Black Horse Agencies)	1.07	1.11

Comparative figures have been re-stated to comply with the new Accounts Regulations

Gross capital comprises subordinated liabilities and subscribed capital, together with reserves – the profits accumulated over many years.

Gross capital as a percentage of shares and borrowings (7.73% at the end of 1998) measures the proportion that the gross capital bears to the Group's liabilities to holders of shares and deposits.

Liquid assets (22.29% of shares and borrowings at the end of 1998) are generally readily available. This enables the Group to meet requests for withdrawals, make new mortgage loans and fund other business activity. Most of the Group's assets are long term mortgages which are not easily convertible into cash, whilst liabilities to investors are in the main repayable on demand or over notice periods of up to 90 days.

The profit for the year as a percentage of mean total assets in 1998 was 0.42%. The profit/assets ratio measures the proportion that the Group's profit after taxation for the year bears to the average of the Group's total assets during the year.

A company needs to pay dividends to equity shareholders, a building society has no such requirements. The Society has made the decision in supporting its mutual stance to minimise profit levels in order to provide further benefits to members primarily by improving interest rates to savers and lowering mortgage rates to borrowers.

Management expenses represent the ordinary costs of running the Group and mainly comprise the cost of staff, buildings and depreciation. Mean total assets are derived from the average Group Balance Sheet over the year.

The ratio of management expenses excluding exceptional items and Black Horse Agencies as a percentage of mean managed total assets has fallen by 4% during 1998 and is considered by the Board to be a comparable measure of business efficiency year on year.

Auditors' statement to the members and depositors of Bradford & Bingley building society

We have examined the summary financial statement set out on pages 1 to 4.

Respective responsibilities of directors and auditors

The summary financial statement is the responsibility of the directors. Our responsibility is to report to you our opinion on its consistency with the full annual accounts, annual business statement and directors' report and its conformity with the requirements of Section 76 of the Building Societies Act 1986 and regulations made under it.

Basis of opinion

We conducted our examination of the statement in accordance with the Auditing Guideline "The auditors' statement on the summary financial statement" adopted by the Auditing Practices Board.

Opinion

In our opinion the summary financial statement is consistent with the full annual accounts, the annual business statement and directors' report of Bradford & Bingley Building Society for the year ended 31st December 1998 and conforms with the requirements of the Building Societies Act 1986 and regulations made under it.

KPMG Audit Plc

Chartered Accountants, Registered Auditor
1 The Embankment
Neville Street
Leeds LS1 4DW
23rd February 1999

Bibliography

Gray, S. J. and Roberts, C. B. *Summary Financial Statements* (1993 ICAEW Research Board)

Evolution of Summary Financial Statements – Practical Experience to Date (1993 ICAEW)

Summary Financial Statements. A Commentary and Guide Deloitte (1990 Coopers & Lybrand)

The Merchant Handbook (1998 Merchant Corporate Design)

Summary Financial Statements. A Survey of Senior Businessmen's Views (1989 Coopers & Lybrand)

Hansford, A., Hussey, J. and Hussey, R. *Corporate Communication. Shareholders' Views of the Annual Review* (1996 Deloitte & Touche)

FRAG 15/95 *Simpler Procedures for Summary Financial Statements* (1995 ICAEW)

Summary Financial Statements – The Way Forward (1996 ICAEW)

Summary Financial Statements Amending Regulations. A Consultative Document (1992 DTI)

FRAG 36/92 *Proposed Amendments to Summary Financial Statements Regulations* (1992 ICAEW)

Consultative Document *Summary Financial Statements for Listed Public Companies* (1989 DTI)

Section 251 Companies Act 1985

The Companies (Summary Financial Statement) Regulations 1990 (SI 1990 No 515)

The Companies (Summary Financial Statement) Regulations 1992 (SI 1992 No 3075)

The Companies Act 1985 (Amendment of Sections 250 and 251) Regulations 1992 (SI 1992 No 3003)

Bibliography

The Companies (Summary Financial Statement) Regulations 1995 (SI 1995 No 2092)

Auditing Guideline *The Auditors' Statement on the Summary Financial Statement* (1991 Auditing Practices Board)

Practice Note 8 *Reports by Auditors Under Company Legislation in the United Kingdom* (1994 Auditing Practices Board)

Practice Note 18 *The Audit of Building Societies in the United Kingdom* (1998 Auditing Practices Board)

SAS 600 *Auditors' Reports on Financial Statements* (1993 Auditing Practices Board)

Index